God's Grand Design

Booklet 1

CREATION

Everything You Wanted to Know About Creation

Directly from Almighty God

Richard Ferguson

God's Grand Design: CREATION by Richard Ferguson
Copyright © 2024 by Richard Ferguson
All Rights Reserved.
ISBN: 978-1-59755-421-3

Published by: ADVANTAGE BOOKS™
                Longwood, Florida, USA
                  www.advbookstore.com

This book and parts thereof may not be reproduced in any form, stored in a retrieval system or transmitted in any form by any means (electronic, mechanical, photocopy, recording or otherwise) without prior written permission of the author, except as provided by United States of America copyright law.

Unless otherwise indicated, Scripture quotations taken from The Holy Bible KING JAMES VERSION (KJV), public domain.

Scriptures marked (NKJV) are taken from the Holy Bible NEW KING JAMES VERSION®. Copyright© 1982 by Thomas Nelson, Inc. Used by permission. All rights reserved.

Library of Congress Catalog Number: 20241938391

Name: Ferguson, Richard, Author
Title: *God's Grand Design: CREATION*
            Richard Ferguson
            Advantage Books, 2024
ISBN: Paperback: 978159754213
Subjects: RELIGION: Christian Life – Inspirational

Evangeline Ferguson: Lead Contributor and Lead Editor

First Printing: June 2024
24 25 26 27 28 29 30   10 9 8 7 6 5 4 3 2 1

God Speaks To His Sacred Children about This Book And Its Author

Our Loving Father's Exact Words Spoken to Me His <u>Anointed Messenger</u>:

"This book is written for you by my special favored son. He is my sacred child, like all of you are. But listen to what he has to say for I approve of His words in this book. He has worked very hard to bring you advanced truths of my creations. Richard is completely right when he describes the spiritual realm and the physical universe. That they are indeed created so all of my sacred children may return to me after the rebellion of Lucifer and the fall of Adam and Eve as is described in your Christian Bible.

Listen to him with both your ears, for Richard has a unique and true understanding of things that are not available to those who believe in me by other means. I, your Father in Heaven, have asked Richard to do something I have never asked any others of my children to do. Listen to him for he is my messenger, and he will help lead you back to me so we may together enjoy eternal life in a paradise each of you can barely imagine. Yet, it is waiting for you.

Richard is one of my special children even before he was born on the Earth. If you listen to what he has to say and read what he has written, that will lead you back to me without fail. I love all of you so very much from the bottom of my heart. Pray to me. Ask me questions about your lives. I will answer you. Be prepared to listen to what I have to say for it will be for your eternal goodness and salvation.

I love you, Your Loving Divine Father

Table of Contents

ABOUT THIS BOOK AND ITS AUTHOR 3

INTRODUCTION 5

BEFORE CREATION 7

OUR MAGNIFICENT STORY BEGINS 7

GOD'S CREATION WE LIVE IN 27

A SCIENTIFIC VIEW OF PHYSICAL CREATION'S DESTINY 46

THE HEAVENLY KINGDOM 51

APPENDIX 1 78

APPENDIX 2 80

Introduction

Author's Note:

My dear brothers and sisters in Christ, I cannot begin to describe what it is like for me to communicate with Our Heavenly Father, Our Lord and Savior Jesus Christ and our Blessed Mother Mary. This is what was needed to write the two books shown below. The enormous love, the kindness, the sincerity, the tenderness, and affection I experience when I have the occasion to speak with the divine goes way beyond any words that attempt to describe it. Sometimes my body even tingles with the ever most pleasurable feelings I never want to end.

Writing the master book, <u>"God's Grand Design of All Creation for Your Redemption"</u> and this booklet, <u>"God's Grand Design, Booklet 1 Creation"</u> has given me the most gorgeous, lovingly warm sensations I've ever felt. I can only imagine how beautiful the Heavenly Kingdom will be for us.

To emphasize this magnificent action taken by Almighty God for our benefit is contained within the master book this booklet and the ones to follow are derived from. The title of the master book is:

God's Grand Design of All Creation for Your Redemption

This booklet titled

"God's Grand Design, Booklet One, Creation"

This is the first in a series of booklets where each one focuses on a particular topic exploring in depth the subject matter indicated in the title drawn from the master book shown above. Booklet number two will be addressing our Blessed Mother Mary.

Booklet #1: CREATION

Content Note:

Our beloved Bible is true and correct created two thousand years ago. This applies to all of the 66 books in the Christian Bible. Throughout our beloved Bible there are no direct words from Almighty God or any other divine person. All the books in the Bible are inspired by our loving Father in Heaven, by Our Lord and Savior Jesus Christ and The Holy Spirit which proceeds from them. The books in our Bible were then written by a host of authors who were inspired directly by God. God's direct words were however never directly written down.

Also, the first part of this booklet contains essential information that mostly has already been published in the master work titled, "God's Grand Design of All Creation for Your Redemption." If you do not have a copy of this book, everything herein will be new to you. Otherwise, the second half of this booklet contains new information never published before, especially what Jesus Christ says about who goes to heaven or not.

Direct Words From Almighty God:

If you are reading this, you're holding the second booklet written containing the exact words spoken to me over the last couple of years by our loving Father, Lord and Savior and our Holy Spirit. This has never happened before in the history of our Father's sacred children. This is you and me. This is what your true identity is. You are a Sacred Child of Almighty God. Contained herein is part of what Our Heavenly Father wants me to communicate to all of His sacred children. I am our Holy Father's Anointed Messenger.

Before Creation

Our Magnificent Story Begins

Many eons ago as we think of it, there was a timeless time when all that existed was the Holy Trinity. The totality of everything we know of was the sacred Holy Trinity. Each of the three persons was infinite and limitless in all ways. Even in ways we as God's sacred children cannot understand. Each was and is pure and perfect and eternally powerful beyond our imagination. Their existence was complete ecstasy, happiness and fulfillment. Their joy and complete fulfillment came with the endless exploration of each other's infinite character, power, and personality. Each has infinite power characterized in diverse ways.

The Trinity needed nothing as they each were complete in and of themselves. And if they so wanted, they could expand outward their exploits in any manner they chose to continue their fulfillment and joy. We as sacred children of God cannot begin to understand or fathom the extent of their infinite love for each other and their limitless power. This is beyond our capability to understand or imagine.

Said a different way, within eons of time before now as we know it you and I did not exist. This is something that it is extremely hard for us to imagine. There was nothingness instead of all of us God's sacred children. Yes, there was complete nothingness that Our Heavenly Father had control over. But…

Booklet #1: CREATION

What is nothingness?

This is an excellent question and to all of God's sacred children it is almost impossible to imagine or understand. One definition of nothingness could be the absence of anything at all. But then what does that mean? It means there is no matter; there are no physical rules because all scientific measurements are not there. There is no time. There is no dimensionality. There is no up or down. There is no potentiality meaning no part of nothingness possesses any possibilities at all.

There can be no understanding because understanding would be something and nothingness means there is the absence of everything including understanding. People picture nothingness as black. Well black is really a color. Color is something therefore nothingness is not black.

There is no time because time is something and nothingness means just that, it is the complete absence of anything related to time. There are no physical laws, nothing at all. The laws of physics or chemistry and so on are completely absent for these laws constitute something which does not exist in nothingness.

I think you get the picture of where creation came from. Also, I think now you have a deeper understanding of the power of Our Heavenly Father, his only begotten son Jesus, and the Holy Spirit, which proceeds from them. What limitless and infinite power they have! They can use nothingness in order to create whatever it is their hearts' desire. They do this by thinking whatever it is into existence. When Aristotle talked about the minds of babies being a tableau Rasa, he had no idea what nothingness is. To him a baby's mind was blank. But even Aristotle who is one of my favorite philosophers, did not understand fully where the idea of a blank mind could be.

Prologue of Sacred Creation:

Many eons ago as we think of it, there was a timeless time when all that existed was the Holy Trinity. The totality of everything we know of was the sacred Holy Trinity. Each of the three is infinite and limitless in all ways they choose to be. Each was powerful beyond imagination. Their existence was complete ecstasy, happiness and fulfillment. Their joy and complete fulfillment came with the endless exploration of each other's infinite character, power, and personality.

The Trinity needed nothing as they each were complete in and of their selves. And if they so choose, they could expand outward their exploits in any manner they chose to continue their fulfillment and joy. Us as children of God cannot really begin to understand or fathom the extent of their infinite love for each other and their limitless power.

We, sacred children of God, learned about ourselves and all creation inside the heavenly realm and outside it as well. We played games with our loving Father. He nurtured us and he told us wonderful stories about the creation to come. It was a wonderland of delight full of joy, happiness, and fulfillment especially when Our Father would teach us about so many delightful things that are yet to come. Our Father's sacred children were happy beyond human description when we would play with our Holy Father and frolic and enjoy with all the other children in the heavenly Kingdom. All of us mature in separate ways. None are the same, all different, as was the will of Our Father.

Over what we now call time, each child grew in separate ways from all the others. Each one of us was becoming a unique one-of-a-kind individual sacred child of God. God does not ever use a cookie-cutter in any of his creations no matter what it may be. Remember, no two trees on earth are the same either. This also

Booklet #1: CREATION

applies to the animal kingdom as well. Although fish seem to be identical to our eyes, they are not identical replications of each other. Each fish is microscopically different in one way or another in spite of their genes being the same.

Remember Almighty God exists independent of time. He knows what will happen in the future in great detail because He is already living there. He is the Alpha and Omega. God knew well in advance of Satan's rebellion. Therefore, as a supreme act of love for his children, God created the spiritual realm and the physical realm which would overlap each other. It must be this way because God created his sacred children with two parts. That is the spiritual way, existing in their minds. And the physical, allowing his children to procreate and provide a pathway for their salvation leading directly back to God in heaven and eternal life with their Father. Please remember again our spiritual bodies extend outward beyond our physical bodies. The only reason for creation is a monumental act of love for God's children to use this pathway back to the origin of their existence in the heaven and eternal life with their heavenly Father.

This Holy creation of God's children occurred after the rebellion of Lucifer against Almighty God and the expulsion of Lucifer now called Satan and all the angels that followed him in his rebellion. Our creation also occurred after Lucifer and his rebel angels were cast down out of the heavenly kingdom to the spiritual realm only and to earth where Satan became the prince of the earth. It is because of the rebellion against God it became necessary all of God's sacred children would need to make a choice now because evil has entered into creation. The choice was one that would determine each of our eternal destinies.

God's Grand Design

What Existed Before Creation

Question: Dear Lord Jesus Christ, what actually existed before you created what we children know of? What was it like when we did not exist yet?

Answer Revealed from Jesus Christ:
September 2023

"Paradise perfect in every way beyond anything you can possibly understand. Yes, the three of us your Almighty Father me, my only begotten son, and the Holy Spirit which connects us all proceeds from us to the dimensions we are contemplating to create.

1. *We love our existence so much we wish to expand to include our children.*
2. *We want them to love us from their hearts, chosen by their free will.*
3. *We have free will to do what pleases us.*
4. *And we want our children to inherit this as well.*
5. *The space and dimensions we live or exist in are endless.*
6. *There are no limitations. Everything is absolute perfection.*

As you described, we live in a timeless way even when it is so easy to create a timeline that if we wish and begin and end at any particular point. If we wanted, we could create a timeline you exist in, and we then could observe how things develop and proceed to their ultimate fruition. We have done this many times before.

If we want something all we need to do is think it into existence. [1]Then we can do with it whatever we choose. Each of us three is an infinite being and complex beyond any kind of your understanding. It gives us great pleasure and joy interacting as we

---

[1] Nothing is impossible for Almighty God

Booklet #1: CREATION

can explore one another in intimate and joyful ways seeing all the different and experience all the endless facets of our personalities and character. Our interaction and exploration of each other can be endless if we choose. What joy, fulfillment, happiness, and ecstasy we experience by doing this together. We have no needs of anything else but the Triad three. [2]

At some timeless point we collectively decided we wanted to create an additional source of pleasure and enjoyment and love for all three of us. We thought into existence the idea of our children, our sacred children who we love as dearly as we love each other. We bestowed upon our children limited talents but enough for them, you, to thrive in the physical realm we have not yet created. We know you will need this because we already know one of our future angels will rebel and then hate our children trying his best to destroy what we lovingly created. Our children are part of us.

This is why there is so much evil in your physical world. This is why we created the physical world because we must go into it, the law of degradation is what your scientists call entropy. Nothing in this world including your physical bodies we thought into existence will be able to exist forever as we do. A time will come all those with freewill we bestowed will become a fork in the path. And

---

[2] Each being of the Trinity that is Almighty God is infinitely complex and joyful for the other two to explore and enjoy. Each member of the Trinity is infinite in their own way, an infinite person. Before our Father created us his sacred children, all three of the Trinity were in a state of ecstasy and pleasure while they explored the infinite facets of each of the other two members of the Trinity. The Trinity in and of itself was in a state of infinite paradise exploring the never-ending beautiful facets of each other. They did not need to create sacred children, which is us. But they chose to do so in order to expand their infinite love and experience that in a different way. Yes, I know how do you expand infinite love? One hint of a complex answer is that they would then be able to experience love in a different way with their sacred children because they would experience their children's love for them in addition to the infinite love of each other. English words cannot describe it any better than this because their love for each other is mysterious and infinite.

some will choose to love your Father, his begotten son me, and the Holy Spirit that binds everything in glorious love and ecstasy.

We already know so very much of each of you who have chosen to with your creator in the perfect paradise we have already created. The others who have rejected us we are so sorrowful about what they will go the way of entropy and dissolve ultimately into nothingness. [3] This is the only kind of pain we have in our hearts but the rebellion of Lucifer with his pride is what created all of this pain and suffering. He will go the way of entropy and ultimately

---

[3] It is these few sentences from our Lord and Savior Jesus Christ that describes what hell really is. Hell is not fire and brimstone. It is not eternal suffering. When you think about this, this description of hell must be true. The reason is simple. Our Almighty Father is love in the purest form. When I speak with our loving Father in heaven, I am always overwhelmed with the sound of his loving voice when he speaks to me. It is pure love, kindness, and intense dedication to me just one and only one of his sacred children on earth. There is a magnificent depth to every word he says to me when we talk. There is a three-dimensional quality in his voice and when I listen to him, it is as if there is no end to the third dimension of what he says to me. It is as if our loving Father has his magnificent arms of love wrapped around me such that I never ever want it to end. I feel like I could spend eternity within his loving arms and his voice saying things like "I love you my dear son". His voice always brings tears to my eyes because of the intensity of his loving words and embrace. I am the luckiest sacred child of God on this earth having been selected as his anointed messenger to all others of his sacred children. So, our loving Father in heaven will separate those that love him from those who choose to reject him. The agony, the intense agony of all those who enter hell is the fact that they know for certain that because of their behavior on earth they will fully understand what they are now missing for all eternity. What is left of their hearts will be in sheer emptiness and agony for they will have experienced for a very short time what true love is when they confronted our Lord and Savior Jesus Christ and are shown all the awful sinful deeds they perpetrated against God's sacred children. So, it is not fire and brimstone. It is worse. They will know what they have turned away from knowing there is no chance they will ever escape hell. There will come a time for all the citizens of hell where they will start to disintegrate which is consistent with the laws of entropy on earth where everything basically falls apart. They too in hell will fall apart and disassemble themselves such that as they disintegrate, they will say their spiritual bodies fall apart and they will reach a point where their minds will slowly stop working in their perceptions of everything will melt into nothingness from which they came. Actually, melting back into nothingness from which they came is an act of love from Our Heavenly Father for he is not one that will make even those that rejected him, he will never force agony upon anybody including those that viciously rejected him and did great damage to his sacred children. As the citizens of hell disintegrate back into nothingness it is an act of kindness from God.

Booklet #1: CREATION

on your timeline we have given you, he too will dissolve into nothingness from whence he came. [4]

On your timeline to mention it is getting short. Our begotten son will return to the physical realm and separate those destined for an existence of perfect ecstasy from those who will ultimately dissolve as your universe will. I cannot express to your limited senses just how much we three love you with all of our hearts. That is such a limited way of saying what we really feel for each of you our children who chose to be with us into eternity which will never end. We love you so very much, my son. We look forward to greeting you and your permanent home with all those whom you love and yes, my son including your doggies that you love so much. [5] *I hope this answers your question about our existence before we started to create different realms to make your existence possible with us in timeless paradise.* [6]

I love you,
Jesus Christ

Note: Some of the above sentences are not grammatically correct. Some of the thoughts are a little discontinuous and need some intelligent interpretation. I left it that way because it was the way I heard it when Jesus spoke to me. I will never change or interpret anything God tells me.

Never in my life had I heard such powerful words spoken to me. Our Lord and Savior did indeed answer all my questions about

---

[4] Astronomers, astrophysicists, and cosmologists are concluding that our universe due to dark energy will expand without end and result in nothingness. This is a mainstream hypothesis.

[5] God knows and understands each of us in magnificent detail. He even knows about my love for my dogs.

[6] God loves us so very much that if He did not create the spiritual realm and importantly the physical realm, we would not be able to be redeemed from sin and not be able to join the Trinity in their timeless realm of infinite joy and fulfillment. More on this later...

God's Grand Design

existence of the Trinity before they started to create realms that would be needed to save us, his children from sin. He explained precisely why they created the different realms I will describe to you in the following pages.

God so loved his children he not only send his only begotten son, [7] he created multiple realms needed for our salvation on an individual basis after Lucifer's rebellion and the fall of Adam and Eve. Yes, God loves us so very much he created us in his image and created this universe we live in. He did this so we can decide through our belief in Him and loving actions to join him in an eternal loving paradise. He also created other realms designed to support our lives on this physical earth to make possible for us to choose our Almighty Father so we can live with Him in paradise for eternity.

So, dear brothers and sisters, remember this.

<u>The entire universe we live in, all the stars and everything else contained within it have been specifically designed and fine-tuned for us and only us to receive redemption from sin if we choose through our own free will.</u>

Yes, dear reader. This also means there are no space aliens. Yes, there are none. So, what about all the UFOs that have been in the news a lot lately? This topic deserves another booklet. However, the short answer involves the fact Satan is the prince of the earth. The earth is his domain Satan, and his demons are what scientists would call multidimensional. The UFOs people see are first off extremely dangerous to any of God's sacred children who physically get too close to them. They are multidimensional which

---

[7] John 3:16 NKJV

explains their fantastic flying characteristics with what we call UFOs. They are not physical. How do I know this? Some time ago I asked Our Lord and Savior Jesus about this. The above is what he told me. Do not be too surprised sometime in the future we will make contact with what we think are alien beings. They are not. They are satanic demons trying to destroy as many of God sacred children as they can.

We sacred children of God are the only reason the entire universe exists. Think of that dear reader and think about how precious you are to Almighty God if He would do all of this for your individual redemption. Our Father in heaven loves us that much and more than we can imagine.

The Fundamental Nature of Creation

This Booklet is the story of creation. It is magnificent and reflects Our Father's deepest love for all his children. Again, this is you. This is one of the sacred truths contained in the book I just mentioned above.

Please realize the world view constantly talked about in our media, in liberal progressive politics, in other high government places is Satanic in its foundations. They only talk about the physical realm and completely ignore the vast majority of existence within the spiritual realm. They ignore the fact all of us sacred children of God are indeed spiritual sacred beings created by our loving Almighty Father in the heavenly kingdom.

Their progressive liberal world view is human centered. They say we know best how to live our lives. God does not exist, and people are expendable. Think of all the throw-away babies in the womb. Since 1971 our country has performed greater than 72 million abortions in America. Satan is controlling our Democrat party that is leading our country into extinction. Think of the tens of millions of illegal aliens Biden has purposely let into our country.

God's Grand Design

Satan wants power over all of God's sacred children. The reason for the invasion of illegal people is one day the Democrats will give these people the power of voting. Satan craves power and so too does the Democrat party. Satan hates our country just like he hates me, God's Anointed Messenger. Our country is the only one on earth that is specifically founded on Judeo-Christian values, principles, and morality.

The Only Two Foundational Forces That Exist within God's Creation

Realize within all creation there are only TWO fundamental forces in all that is seen and unseen. These two foundational forces are diametrically opposed to each other and exist within all creation. What are these two forces?

First, there is the infinite love of Almighty God. There is our loving Father Almighty. He loved all his sacred children into existence billions of years ago. Yes, I said billions. You existed within the heavenly kingdom before you personally chose to come to earth and take the earth test. More on the earth test later. But remember this surprising fact; our Holy Father loved us all into existence long before this earth was created. Think about that! The first force in all creation is Love. It is love that brings all of God's sacred children together in harmony and happiness. Love is what joins God's sacred children with our loving heavenly Father.

There is our Lord and Savior Jesus Christ. Yes, he really did save the world and provided a direct path for all of us to go back to the Heavenly Kingdom from where we came. Then there is the Holy Spirit which proceeds from the Father and the Son. The Holy Spirit is what glues all of reality together. From these holy sacred persons within the Trinity, they are the source of all infinite love for each and every one of you.

Booklet #1: CREATION

Contained in this small booklet, is true information Our Heavenly Father wants each and every sacred child of His (YOU) to understand. We as God's sacred children will then understand our true identity and where we really come from. This includes why we are on this earth. Our Heavenly Father answers these questions and many more.

This booklet speaks to God's creation of the reality all of us live in. This Godly truth is far from what you hear on the news or other sources governed by the rich elite among us. All of that is based on satanic foundations. No bigger lie has ever existed in all of human history than what all of us here constantly in our news media and other liberal and communist sources.

We've grown accustomed to this satanic atmosphere, our Satan poisoned earth, it's increasingly hard believing anything we see or hear whether it is on TV, in printed format or even from people we call friends. We are at the point in our society where to trust someone is mostly equated to a fool's journey with a bad ending. Our Father in heaven knows this even far better than each of us does ourselves.

This is one reason our Loving Father has provided to us, His sacred children, advanced knowledge of all existence within His creations spiritual and physical. Our Father has asked me to be His Anointed Messenger. I said "Yes!" to our loving Father in Heaven.

Our physical existence on earth, why?

All physical existence on earth has three purposes:
1. So, all God sacred children may experience their Father in a new and different way.
2. To provide all God's sacred children a direct pathway back into the Heavenly Kingdom from where we were before we were born to earth.

God's Grand Design

3. To provide Our Heavenly Father's only begotten son a way to bring together the physical and the sacred spiritual life. How we live our lives is what determines whether we qualify to reenter the Heavenly Kingdom. Simply follow these three rules of Godly existence.
   a) Love God first above everything else in your life on earth.
   b) Love all your Neighbors as you love yourself. This means everybody.
   c) Love your enemies, treat your enemies as you want to be loved and treated.

I Became Our Heavenly Father's Anointed Messenger for a Specific Reason.

This booklet will contain words that have been directly spoken to me by Almighty God, be it Our Heavenly Father or Jesus Christ. I am your Heavenly Father's Anointed Messenger. Yes, God does speak with me your author directly so I may transcribe the words spoken and publish them for your benefit.

As Our Heavenly Father's anointed messenger, I have been gifted by the Holy Trinity with certain spiritual gifts and capabilities that are not necessarily normal within human life on earth. I was not always God's anointed messenger. This revelation occurred a number of years ago much to my personal surprise. Our Heavenly Father asked me to be his anointed messenger to all his sacred children on earth and to write a book that contained his personalized message to all his sacred children. I answered yes, I will. I did not have any clear idea about what I said yes to. But I knew through my love of God and faith whatever it would be is something exceptionally good. So, I said yes.

I do not want to get into all the details about how this happened, the history of why this happened and things like that. To

Booklet #1: CREATION

summarize some gifts bestowed upon me, they include the ability to have two-way conversations with Our Father in Heaven, Our Lord and Savior Jesus Christ and the Holy Spirit, which proceeds from them. In addition, I am so blessed to be able to converse also with our Blessed Mother Mary whom I love very dearly. The next booklet I am writing as you read this is all about our Blessed Mother Mary and her apparitions that communicated much information regarding the end times and what will happen. She told me everything.

Using what I call spiritual vision, I am able to see the image of Jesus Christ and Blessed Mother Mary. Both Jesus and Mary are my constant companions every minute of every day and they know my thoughts and my feelings about things where I do not even have to express them. They already know because they are so intimately close to me.

Our Heavenly Father once told me he knows my thoughts before I do. Please think about that as it relates to your own life and the closeness Our Heavenly Father has to each of his sacred children. What a wonderfully loving thing to have. Our Father loves each of us so much that when we were created, he left a little bit of himself within our personal spiritual being. It is never a case of "I am here, and God is there." In the Psalms, once wrote that no matter where he goes, Our Heavenly Father is already there with him.[8]

What Are We as God's Sacred Children?

Yet, it is out of nothingness our loving Almighty Father created each and every one of us His sacred children in the blink of an eye. Additionally, when all of us were created, each sacred child was different than any other child in all of us that were created. All of us were completely loved by God equally yet at the same time no

---

[8] Psalm 139:7-12, You Can't Hide From God - Wellspring Christian Ministries

two of us were alike. Every one of us was different from every other one of us. We were all given the gift of being unique.

At one moment within this timeless time before creation the Trinity thought it would be a magnificent idea to create special and sacred children in their own image. And so, they did. It was an extraordinarily complex task to create spiritual children made in their image. There was much discussion about what characteristics and power their sacred children would possess. One particularly important power is that of free will. This gift is enormously powerful, and it is something all of us use every day of our earthly lives. All of us could choose what we wished and pursue that or change our minds and do something different. The power of free will is great and along with our choices comes natural consequences.

We are all created by the limitless loving Trinity, the Father, the only begotten son, and the Holy Spirit which proceeds from them. We, as their children, were given some limited powers of the Holy Trinity. But most importantly, we were given the power to love and to communicate with our Holy Almighty Father, his only begotten son, and the Holy Spirit.

Our Holy Trinity loves us so very much Our Father designed the creation of his children and the realms so they are within the very core of our very own physical and spiritual being. Yes, all of God's sacred children were created with two parts, our spiritual being which is directly connected to the spiritual realm and Almighty God. People completely ignore this fact. Yet, it's determinative and true Our Heavenly Father loved us so much that when all of us were created in the blink of an eye, Our Father left some of himself within our spiritual being.

This is so because Our Father, his only begotten son, and the Holy Spirit which proceeds from them, would be able to experience

Booklet #1: CREATION

every detail of our lives. This was and remains a magnificent gift to each of us for this unending connection to God allows us to communicate with the divine very easily. It allows us to pray to God and ask questions, ask what is needed for each of us.

Because Our Father left a part of himself within our spiritual being, this allows the Trinity to know everything about who we are, our personalities, and everything we've said or done while on the earth. Said differently, one thing everybody does not know regarding our existence on earth is Our Father in heaven knows every thought we have every motivation every emotion and everything we say and do. It is in this way; they can experience everything we do while we exist on earth and elsewhere. Whatever it is we experience in our lives, the Trinity also experiences. The Holy Trinity knows every detail within our minds, everything we say and do while on this earth and even every detail of our physical bodies.

One time a number of months ago when I was speaking with our Holy Father, he told me he knew my thoughts before I did. Think about this dear sacred child of God. Our Father loves us so much he wants to experience what we do into the finest of detail. In a very real sense, the divine is intimately connected with us every moment of our lives and is ready and able to answer any of our questions and guide us throughout our entire lives.

What Does It Mean When I Say God Is Within Each Of Our Spiritual Bodies?

It Means That Secrets Are Impossible

Our Almighty Father, who created all of us sacred children, loves us so much he left a part of himself within our spiritual bodies. He is with us personally every moment of every day. Additionally, he designed the spiritual realm such that nothing is hidden in any way.

There are absolutely no secrets within the spiritual realm, nor should there ever be for our Father is not like that in any way. Said differently, Our Father in Heaven is not limited in any way throughout all of his creations. Like the Psalms say, "no matter where I go you dear Father, you are always there."

I have to say to everybody it is impossible for the cosmos or any other part of creation to contain any kind of secret anywhere at all. Everything is just transparent. This comes as a massive surprise for all the crooks on earth when they die and have their life review. All the secrets they thought they kept from everybody else are plain to see in great detail. They will be held accountable for everything they did to everybody else on planet Earth.

Remember all of us individually are designed with two parts to each of us, the physical part and the spiritual part. It is the spiritual part of our eternal spiritual being that is eternal. There is no end to our spiritual being. Our spiritual lives represent and participate in a continuum of existence that has no end. There is only one condition on this eternal existence. That is, it depends on how well we followed Our Heavenly Father's rules of existence. This is covered in another section of this booklet 1. On the other hand, the physical part of us, which many believe is all there is, has a limited existence. And over time, will slowly disintegrate due to the laws of entropy in the universe. It takes a while but each of us will notice that the individual parts of our physical body stopped working very well. This is called aging, and everybody tries to avoid the slow disintegration of our bodies which is completely unavoidable.

A Note after Our Creation

You and I are the sacred spiritual children of Almighty God, Our Holy Father who loves each and every one of us. After Our Father created all his children, for an undetermined length of time all of us would stay with the Trinity in the Heavenly Kingdom. We stayed

Booklet #1: CREATION

with the Holy Trinity for unknown eons of time as we would measure it today. It is here we children would be nurtured, loved, explore the Heavenly realm, and play with our Almighty Father in so many different ways. We also learned about the values given by Our Father. This includes all his characteristics and personality and his unlimited love.

This gave Our Father such infinite joy and happiness to be with his children. Additionally, this time for us within the Kingdom of Heaven before we were born into the physical earth, gave us time to learn. Gave us time to learn about Our Almighty Father, to learn about his creation, to learn about ourselves and mature in the direction of the talents and personal characteristics Our Father intended for each of us. Remember, each child is individually unique. No two are the same.

We learned about ourselves and all creation inside the Heavenly realm and outside it as well. We played games with our loving Father. He nurtured us and he told us wonderful stories about the creation to come. It was a wonderland of delight full of joy, happiness, and fulfillment especially when Our Father would teach us about so many delightful things that are yet to come. Regarding playing various kinds of games with Our Heavenly Father, we learned that trying to play hide and seek never worked. Remember, Our Heavenly Father is already everywhere! Is that cheating? I do not know how to score that one. Our Father's sacred children were happy beyond human description when we would play with him and frolic and enjoy with all the other children in the Heavenly Kingdom. All of us mature in separate ways, none of us the same, all different, as is the will of Our Father.

Over what we now call time, each child grew in diverse ways from all the others. Each one of us was becoming a unique one-of-a-kind

God's Grand Design

individual child of God. God does not ever use a cookie-cutter in any of his creations no matter what it may be.

Why God Created Creation.

Remember Almighty God exists independent of time. He knows what will happen in the future in great detail because he is already living there. He is the Alpha and Omega. All three loving members of the Trinity live outside of the timeline in which all of their sacred children do live in right now. God knew full well in advance of Satan's coming rebellion. God also knew Eve would be fooled by Satan, and she would lie to Adam so as for him to also eat from the forbidden fruit of the knowledge of good and evil.

Therefore, as a supreme act of love for his children, God created the spiritual realm and the physical realm which would overlap each other. It must be this way because God created his sacred children with two parts. There's the spiritual part, which exist in our minds. And the physical part, which allows us to procreate and provide a pathway for their salvation and all subsequent generations leading directly back to God in Heaven and eternal life with Our Father.

<u>The reason for all creation is a monumental act of love for God's children. It is to use this pathway back to the origin of our existence in the Heavenly realm and life with Our Heavenly Father for all eternity.</u>

It is not a coincidence in any way all of us, Our Heavenly Father's sacred children, have two separate parts to us. It is the physical part so we can procreate subsequent generations on earth and allow them to have the same opportunity of reuniting with Our Heavenly Father in the heavenly Paradise. Our minds are what contain our spiritual identity, and it is this part of us those lives in a timeless

Booklet #1: CREATION

continuum of life. That is as long as we follow Our Heavenly Father's rules for life on earth which I have already shown above.

The title of the book, "God's Grand Design of All Creation for Your Redemption," is a revelation of a fundamental truth of our existence. Our loving Father in heaven created and expanded the spiritual realm and a completely new physical realm for one purpose and one purpose only. The title of the book listed above is the reason for all creation. It is a magnificent title that is very explanatory why everything we see, feel, touch, think about was created for the direct benefit of all God's sacred children. Without creation there would be no chance that God sacred children would be able to be redeemed. Our redemption is exactly why God created the different realms, spiritual realm, and the physical realm we call the universe and both parts of our physical bodies, the spiritual part in the physical part. This allows each of us to make the choice of whether we wish to go the way of hateful Satan or go the way of our loving Father in heaven.

God's Creation We Live In

In The Beginning

For all of us sacred children of God it is impossible for us to really understand where this book begins. It begins with the testimony of our Almighty Father in the Heavenly Kingdom when he describes a timeless time when only the Trinity existed in luxurious ecstasy exploring the infinite other. That is explained elsewhere within this Booklet 1, Creation. Before the creation we live in now there was the infinite Trinity, God our Father, God our lord and Savior Jesus Christ and the Holy Spirit which proceeds from them. They were exploring the magnificent and infinite dimensions of each other with limitless love and grandeur. Then at some point of timeless time the three decided they wanted to share what they had. They wanted to increase their joy and fulfillment by creating sacred children made in their own image. And so that would come to be.

And so, the beginning for all of us sacred children of God… it began!

Were There Other Creations?

As a note, Our Heavenly Trinity is indeed three infinite persons. Each one is different yet the same. Our Father, our creator during infinite times and what we would call the past has indeed created other creations. The creation we live in is completely different than any of the others Our Father created in unknown times past. The differences between different creations are so great it makes no sense. And they give us no benefit to even begin to try to understand the infinite nature of our loving Father that has created other creations. In fact, Jesus told me that knowing the characteristics of God's other creations would actually harm us. All of the other is completely separated from us in all ways.

Booklet #1: CREATION

They are completely separate in every way. They are not accessible to us residing in our own creation. They are completely not understandable and have no commonality with us. So as Jesus Christ told me when I asked him this question he said:

Jesus Christ
September 30, 2022, 9:46 AM

Yes, my dear son, there are other forms of life within the created realms your Father has done. However, they have no impact on your lives and the trajectory of your existence. The best word to describe this is you are separated from other forms of life. This is a very good thing! Because knowledge of other forms of life necessarily means you will be exposed to the knowledge of different sets of the laws of physics. As well as different situations these other kinds of children of God are dealing with completely separate from your own.

Everything about any other kinds of children of God are very foreign and almost always from your existence. Hence, there is no benefit for you to know anything about the other dimensions, the other forms of life. If you did know something, it would be detrimental to your spiritual path back to us in the Trinity and especially your infinite loving Almighty Father.

"My dear son, there is no benefit in pursuing any understanding of the other creations of your Father. In fact, they can do you harm. This is because as you just said there is no commonality, and they are completely foreign to you with completely different purposes you have no hope of understanding. They do not interact with the creation in which you reside. So, forget they even exist and concentrate on your loving existence in your Father's creation meant especially for you his sacred children made in our image."

Our Father, our creator during infinite times and what we would call the past has indeed created other creations. The creation we live

God's Grand Design

in is completely different than any of the others Our Father created in unknown times past. The differences are so great it makes no sense and gives no benefit to even begin to try to understand the infinite nature of our loving Father that has created other creations.

They are completely separate in every way. They are not accessible to us in our creation. They are completely not understandable and have no commonality with us. Our loving Father created the heavens and the earth; he created all that is seen and unseen. This is a beautiful description of our loving Father creating the creation all of us live in. The creation as described in Genesis of all that is seen and unseen has a specific purpose.

Before all of God's sacred children were loved into existence in the blink of an eye, the Trinity created the heavens and the earth. What am I talking about? In more detail than you have experienced before this includes the following:

1. An expanded spiritual realm. This is to accommodate hell and all of its future residents that get there by rejecting Almighty God through their actions on earth.

2. The physical realm which we call the universe astronomers study to this day. A remarkably interesting fact regarding our physical universe is it is expanding faster than the speed of light. This makes it so the confirmed age of our universe is 13.8 billion years old. But the farthest stars we can see with the James Webb space telescope are twice that distance as expressed in billions of years. The farthest stars are 35.6 billion light years away from us.

3. An incredibly special place was created within our physical universe we call earth. This planet Earth had to meet a detailed specific criterion in order to support our human designed

physical bodies. There is only one planet in the entire universe that met all the requirements to support human life for the necessary minimum amount of time that allows our physical bodies to thrive on this planet. This planet must reside within a certain small area of the entire universe that is stable enough to allow human life for the minimum amount of time before it degrades into a hostile environment. Such things as its position within the galaxy. Positioned so radiation is kept at low levels for life, its position within the galaxy that promotes just the right amount of gravitation and space from other stars. Stars that would otherwise interfere with God's plan for human life. Dr. Hugh Ross[9] of "The Reason to Believe" website has gone to great lengths with his astrophysical team to identify all the necessary requirements for human life throughout the universe. He has written multiple books on this topic I encourage you to read. There is a lot of detail here but sufficed to say our physical bodies and the characteristics of planet Earth have a complex and beautifully integrated symbiotic relationship.

One simple example is carbon dioxide that is hated by the progressive left politicians is actually an attack against the sacred plan of Almighty God for his sacred children. Why? Carbon dioxide is actually what is accurately called the gas of life itself. When we breathe in the air, we take in oxygen to live. When we exhale, we emit carbon dioxide because our bodies need the oxygen that supports life and our lives exhale carbon dioxide which is hated by the progressive left political morons.

---

[9] Reasons to Believe - Home

God's Grand Design

Right now if you take 1,000 molecules of air. There will be only four molecules of carbon dioxide, yes that is scientifically correct, only four molecules of carbon dioxide. If carbon dioxide levels decrease to only two molecules per thousand molecules of air, all life on earth would cease to exist. All of God's sacred children would die and not be able to fulfill the entire purpose of coming to earth. We are only two molecules per thousand of carbon dioxide away from Earth becoming a dead planet. Yet this is what the insane Democrat leftist political party wants to do to us. Satan wants to destroy all of God's sacred children. This is a great way to do it through the politics of our Democrat party.

In my personal view, given there are only two fundamental forces in creation - love and hate. This reduction of carbon dioxide can only be described as satanic hate against God's plan of abundant life for all his sacred children.

If anything, we are in a carbon dioxide drought. Nobody ever mentions the fact plant life has been increasing on planet Earth because of the slight increase in carbon dioxide over the last one hundred years. This simply means more food. It is politically incorrect to even mention this fact for it goes against the Democrat progressive socialist agenda of controlling all citizens through the excuse of carbon dioxide control.

Politically speaking, Democrats are using the lies of saying carbon dioxide is a poison to institute dictatorial socialist government that entirely removes our fundamental human rights as God's sacred children.

Booklet #1: CREATION

4. The holy design of our bodies on earth was established in the heavenly kingdom by all three members of the Holy Trinity. Without getting into too much biology there are two major aspects to each and every one of us sacred children of God.

Jesus Christ
July 30, 2022, 5:28 PM
Remember my son the creation of the physical realm and the spiritual realm is matched perfectly with the design of your human body. This is so the needs of your physical body are met with the resources available to you on earth. And as I said before, it is your brain and the overlying spiritual body you have that is completely in tune with the spiritual realm.

a) Our spiritual being that resides in our physical bodies. It is our spiritual being that has a direct connection with Almighty God. Remember that when all of us were created in the blink of an eye, Our Heavenly Father left a part of him within our spiritual bodies. He loved us so much he did this so we could pray to him. We could ask him questions. We could ask for certain favors to be done for us. Our connection to Almighty God which does include, Father, son, and Holy Spirit. We can indeed communicate with Almighty God. And if we ask questions, it is certain our questions will be answered. We just have to be alert as to the way in which God answers our questions. Our Heavenly Father is everywhere within his creation of all that is seen and unseen.

b) Specifically, the special part of him exists within our spiritual minds. Unfortunately, this is also the place Satan has access to as well. This lays the groundwork for our fundamental task on earth. The task is simple but profound. Do we choose to love Almighty God or do we choose to love

God's Grand Design

ourselves first in agreement with Satan's desires. The answer to this question will determine where we go, heaven or hell.

c) Because we are all spiritual beings before, we came to earth and inhabited our physical bodies; this makes us susceptible to Satan and his demons. They too are spiritual beings. It is in this way, when I was in my mid 30's; I was attacked three separate times personally by Satan himself. A YouTube video was made that describes in detail the three separate times Satan himself attacked me. The title of the video is "<u>Satan Attacks Sacred Child of God</u> ". Now, I am forced to conduct spiritual warfare with Satan and his demons every day of my life. Satan is so clever many of God sacred children do not even realize they are being manipulated through fear by Satan and his demons.

This next thought is extremely important to understand and remember.

Satan Controls His Kingdom By Hatred And Fear!

Whenever someone tries to control you by fear or threats of some kind you know for certain the foundational element is always Satanic. Our government is completely full of these kinds of people. Democrats call this "executive mandates," no democratic process involved! This is how Democrats pushed climate change on us and EV cars that cost our auto companies many billions of losses.

a) The fact Satan controls his Kingdom by hatred and fear is once you think about it is quite obvious. Keep in mind also please that hatred and fear also is observed on individual and personal levels.

b) The one person that comes to mind regarding hatred and fear is my own Father. He was a tyrannical man in all

33

respects. He used great gobs of fear against me when I was growing up. I was made to feel like I was intruding on "his" house. He passed away a number of years ago. Then he made four separate appearances to me by coming out of the floor and rising up two or three feet above floor level. Each time I commanded him in the name of Jesus Christ to "go back to hell where you belong in the name of my Savior and Lord Jesus Christ." Instantly I observed him sinking back into the floor not to be seen again.

On the other hand:

Our Loving Almighty Father Controls His Kingdom By Pure Limitless Love.

a) It is our spiritual bodies that have eternal life. When we die it is only our physical bodies that stop functioning, decay, and return to dust from which they came. Our spiritual bodies then separate from our physical bodies because our spiritual bodies have eternal life as willed by Almighty God. However, do we go to heaven or hell? That depends on how we live our lives. There is another section within this booklet that describes how we must live our lives in order to achieve returning back into the heavenly kingdom.

b) Our physical bodies are the last part of creation. Jesus once told me it took the trinity a long time to decide what the characteristics would be for God's sacred children on earth. The primary characteristic for all of us is the power of free will. Each of us has the power to choose what we do, what we think and what we believe while on earth. It is this free will Satan loves to attack. He loves to make sin appear like an incredibly fun and fulfilling thing. This is how he lures people to sin against Our Heavenly Father, the Trinity and ultimately go to hell as a result. Each of us must stick remarkably close to the rules of life Our Father has laid down for us.

c) If we reject God's rules of life through the manner in which we live our lives, God cannot save us, and we will go to hell. We must also ask for forgiveness for our sins, pray to Almighty God every day and ask for his guidance in everything we say and do. If we do this our lives will go much smoother, and we will be far happier as a result. And when the time comes to meet with our Lord and Savior Jesus Christ for our life review, both you and Jesus will be incredibly happy when he admits you to the heavenly kingdom.

When all of the above was accomplished, it is then God created Adam and Eve and placed them in what today we call the Garden of Eden. Both Adam and Eve were sinless and innocent. They both were very naïve. Our Father gave them one rule, "do not eat the fruit of the tree that contains knowledge of good and evil. If you do this, you will certainly die". Well, they did that. As a result, they were thrown out of the Garden of Eden, a paradise intended for all of God's children that wanted to come to earth and experience living in the physical realm. Had Eve not been fooled by Satan and disobeyed our loving Father, the entire story of all of us sacred children of God would be very much different. When Eve lied to Adam about the fruit of the forbidden tree, both of them created hell on earth.

Now, the above story of Adam and Eve is objective history. It is not a myth the haters of God want you to believe. They really did exist in a paradise like garden. How do I know this? I know this because I am our Loving Father's Anointed Messenger. I have been gifted with the ability to speak directly to our Father in heaven. And when he wishes, he can speak to me wherever I am at the time.

Booklet #1: CREATION

Our Holy Father Speaks To Me

One example of this: I was on a flight from San Francisco to Manila Philippines. We were crossing the middle of the Pacific Ocean, and I was thinking about creation. Suddenly Our Heavenly Father started talking to me. He wanted to tell me something is about my previously authored a book titled, "<u>God's Grand Design of All Creation for Your Redemption</u>." My publisher suggested we change the title so as to make the book appeal to more of the young people in our society.

Our loving Father told me changing the title was not according to his will. He wanted the title I created which is mentioned above. Okay, I will make it exactly that way and I did.

An attack by Satan just occurred a few seconds before our loving Father started to speak to me while I am in my seat in the airplane halfway across the Pacific Ocean. Ask yourself one question by the way. How did God know where I was? How did Satan know too?

This is what our loving Father told me on that occasion. The below text in bold italicized font is part of what he told me on that occasion.

December 2, 2023
Our Loving Almighty Father in Heaven

"That was Satan; he wants to scare you as much as he can. He does not understand your intense love and how much of a fighter you are...

Your publisher has every good intention in changing the title. But it is my will the first book you yourself created is the one that will succeed.

Go with that one my dearest son. So, I will be with you every second of every day. Speak freely in your own way the truth I have given you. I will guide you and Jesus your Savior will guide you

and be with you every moment of every day. You have my highest of blessings.

I love you, my dearest son.

And yes, I want you to use your true title: My Anointed Messenger.

It is things like this I experienced quite often in my life. I am blessed more than I could ever imagine.

Satan Attacks Your Author Three Times

Regarding the tendency toward sin, I know Satan personally! This is an accurate statement due to all the times he has attacked me in so many different ways. I have written about this before but quickly, Satan attacked me personally on three separate occasions about 40 years ago. He attacked me in the middle of the night while my wife and I were sleeping soundly. There was a loud crashing sound, a combination of symbols banging together and a sound like a car hitting our house at high speed. Needless to say, it woke me up. Like many spiritual events, my wife did not hear a thing, nor did she say anything.

When I looked around the dark room who do I see at the foot of the bed, a 7-foot-tall black creature that started leaning over my bed and stare at me with bright red eyes? It was when I saw this horrifying black creature leaning over the foot of my bed; I had to look up at this awful thing, awful black creature. Then, Satan then yelled at me these words: **"I WILL GET YOU; I WILL GET YOU, I WILL GET YOU."** His voice was low and it sounded like rocks banging together in a gravel pit. It was so loud I thought the neighbors certainly heard everything. Satan was yelling at me.

Needless to say, I was scared out of my pajamas. But it did not take too much time for me to recover from this. And now I am forced to conduct spiritual warfare every day of my life because Satan knows I am God's <u>Anointed Messenger</u> to all of his sacred

Booklet #1: CREATION

children. I get attacked by Satan 5 to 6 times a day when he forcefully interrupts my thought process by saying horrific swearwords against the Holy Trinity, against Jesus Christ in particular. At this point he is more of an irritant than anything else. I am no longer scared of Satan at all. Jesus and the heavenly angels protect all of God's sacred children from any harm Satan and his demons try to impose upon us.

The Poem of Evil

Satan Rebels and Attacks God's Children:

But Satan saw and hated them down to his very core.

Our Father knew, before creation, hateful Satan would make horrible war.

Across all dimensions of time, he would try to destroy all he abhorred.

God's children became Satan's target.

Clever and deceitful, his demons roamed finding those to annihilate.

Choose God or Satan, which is our choice always to make.

Our purpose in life here on earth, learn to love or fall into hate.

Live your life as Jesus told, reject Satan and his deathly fate!

The first creation so very special indeed, built for sinners just like you, just like me.

To create a universe for all to pass his test, just love and accept his infinite glory.

Given a choice in this first creation, to God the forgiven we will certainly go.

Or to Satan all sinners will be condemned to flow.

On earth a planet fine-tuned for us, a path to our Father and spiritually grown.

God's Grand Design

These are the creations, meant only for us, a path to God and our eternal home.

The Earth Test

Without creation, a.k.a. the physical realm, God's sacred children wouldn't have the capability, the possibility, the chance of exploring themselves and making the eternal choice between Our Loving Father in heaven and Satan in hell. It is our behavior on earth that determines which one is our eternal destiny.

Our Bifurcated Bodies

You see, remember each of us have two parts to us, our physical bodies and our spiritual bodies. It is our spiritual bodies that contained our minds which reside within the spiritual realm. Our spiritual bodies extend outward and beyond our physical bodies. They are part of the spiritual realm where Our Heavenly Father exists.

Satan also exists within the spiritual realm along with all of his demons some of which were the original angels that rebelled against God untold eons of time ago. They were all kicked out of heaven in the blink of an eye. It was pride and narcissism of Lucifer a high angel in heaven that spelled rebellion against God. They rejected our loving Almighty Father. This quickly turned into horrific hate against our loving Father in heaven and hate against anybody or anything that is associated with Almighty God.

Our Lord and Savior Jesus Christ also experienced a bifurcated human body. Unlike us, where we are half human and half sacred spiritual beings, our Lord and Savior Jesus Christ was different. He too was fully God and fully human. We, sacred children of Our Heavenly Father, are in no way Gods. But we do have our minds that are connected to the spiritual realm. And thus this gives us access to Our Heavenly Father, our Lord and Savior Jesus Christ

Booklet #1: CREATION

and the Holy Spirit which proceeds from them. It is in this way we are able to pray to Almighty God and our Blessed Mother Mary.

The unfortunate aspect of our spiritual minds is this also opens the door to satanic influences. Satan is exceptionally good at tempting people through their spiritual minds. Because of this, most sacred children of God do not make it back into the heavenly kingdom. Each of us sacred children of Almighty God are tempted every day of our lives to depart from our loving Father's rules for our existence and our return to the heavenly kingdom.

In my case, because I am our Father's anointed messenger, I was attacked on three separate occasions by Satan himself. And every day I engage in spiritual warfare against Satan when he attacks me and his disgusting demons as well. This happens to me these three or four times every day. Satan's hatred for me personally is horrifically ugly and disgusting.

There are only a few of God's sacred children in Heaven that choose to take the earth test. Coming to earth is a big deal, a very big deal in the Holy Kingdom. This test is to determine how well we can defeat Satan and follow Almighty God's rules for our existence, our behavior. No one goes to the heavenly kingdom without being pure and perfect. Yes, all of us are sinners. But as long as we do not reject Our Heavenly Father and his rules of existence, we can then go through a purification process, which is most lovely and loving. A process that will wash us clean of any residual satanic influences we picked up along the way in our earthly lives.

Remember, all of us are given the opportunity to come to earth and take what is known in the heavenly Kingdom as the" earth test." Remember also, our loving Father never forces any of his sacred children to do anything. He honors our free will enormously. Always remember our loving Father is not a tyrant, he honors our free will. For those who choose not to take the earth test, they are not penalized in any way. Their actions are interpreted as they love Our Heavenly Father so very much, they will do nothing that could jeopardize that relationship. Their thought process is simply they do not want to risk losing their place in the heavenly kingdom. They remain full and honored citizens of the kingdom of heaven.

For all those who choose to come to earth and take the earth test, they are indeed placing themselves at risk of succumbing to Satan's temptations and living their life rejecting their heavenly Father. For those who do not pass the earth test, they will indeed go to hell. For those who come to earth and take the earth test and succeed retaining their love for Almighty God, they will be rewarded immensely in the heavenly kingdom. For they have proved beyond doubt Satan cannot tempt them.

Remember none of this would have been necessary but is because of the rebellion of Lucifer many eons before our Father loved all of us into existence in the blink of an eye. Coming to earth provides each sacred child of God much valuable information regarding our fundamental character. It also provides information regarding our fundamental ability to love our Father and all others of his sacred children and to forge new relationships with others of God sacred children as well. These relationships will continue on for all eternity.

Before We Are Born To Earth

Each sacred child of God must go through a lengthy process of adaptation and learning new information about earth we as our Father's sacred children never knew before as citizens of heaven. Simply put, earth is radically different from the heavenly kingdom where we spent all of our existence after God loved us into being.

Booklet #1: CREATION

The planet Earth is thoroughly satanically poisoned with sin and rejection of Almighty God. Our earth is poisoned so badly that as we live our day-to-day lives, we usually do not even notice the horrific sinful structures we live in. It is only noticeable when you put God first in your life and when you pray to Almighty God and ask for his loving guidance. It is then you will be guided by God in everything you say and do. And in the process of doing that you will become extremely sensitive to the ways of Almighty God versus the ways of this pathetic Satan poisoned world we live in.

Sin has so saturated earth we are living here like fish in the sea. What I mean by this is fish do not know they are wet. Think about this. Fish do not know they are wet because that is all they know. When we are born to this earth after a small length of time as small children, we start to get increasingly acclimated to the awful sinful ways that exist on this earth. Pretty soon we stop noticing just how sinful things are like the fish not knowing how wet they are.

So, while we are still in the heavenly kingdom, a lot of effort is put into designing the typical characteristics of what life we will have on earth for us. It is a detailed process as described below.

Jesus Christ
September 30, 2022, 9:46 AM

"It is a lengthy process, my dear son. No need for now to go into the selection process of who of God's spiritual children will be the ones next to go to the physical earth. That is a process that is incredibly detailed and arranged to meet the needs and preferences of each child while they are in the Heavenly Kingdom. After the selection process is completed and agreed on that their coming life on the earth will satisfy the spiritual needs of each child. And also, after it is agreed to that their position and location on the earth will be fair.

This means to reveal what their true feelings are, like wanting to come back to the Heavenly realm for all eternity. Or choose to be with Satan in a completely disordered manner where there is no morality or any other fundamental behavioral standards that are to be met. Those who want that will choose Satan with the understanding that at some point in their future they will, as you point out about entropy, will slowly dissolve back into nothingness from which they came.

After the selection process is completed to meet the individual needs of the children of God, they will then need to go through a preparation process next. This includes many things such as acclimatizing them for a life in the physical realm. Remember, none of God's children have any idea what that is like for having been spirit beings for their entire existence. They must get used for example to not have what they want instantaneously. They have to understand what hardship and satanic dishonesty are. Because they have never experienced that either.

They will not understand the experience of dishonesty and other features of the disaster Satan has brought to the earthly realm. This is why little children on earth believe everything they are told and are so gullible to all the falsity that exists on earth.

It is a big deal when one of God's sacred children decides to take the earth test. From the above paragraphs you get a good idea of how complex the preparations are for each individual life before that individual sacred child is born to this earth.

Once we enter the heavenly kingdom, there is zero chance we would ever sin in any way no matter how small it may be. All those tendencies are completely washed away never ever to return again. This is why when I asked Jesus Christ the question, "once we are in heaven is there any chance, we might fall out?" Our Lord told me

Booklet #1: CREATION

directly, "*no.*" It is because we are made pure and perfect during the purification process all of us will go through before we are admitted to the heavenly kingdom.

After taking the earth test and when each of us returned to the spiritual realm we encounter our Lord and Savior Jesus Christ. At this time, he conducts a life review with us. This is the fork in the road for all of us. Either we are destined for heaven or condemned to hell. If we are destined for heaven than the Catholic Church has taught since the 1,400's we all will go to purgatory to receive additional punishment for our sins. Purgatory is not biblical!

Purgatory's punishment is administered by the angels from the heavenly kingdom. This is a Catholic Church doctrine and is not true. This was invented by what was called back then in the Middle-Ages, the magisterium. The bishops and cardinals had a consciousness that it was not enough suffering on earth to pay for all of our sins including original sin. So, they invented an additional place called purgatory where all of us must go and suffer more before we enter into the kingdom of God.

As Jesus has told me a number of separate times, "*there is no purgatory.*" Our loving Father is not in the business of making his sacred children suffer needlessly. Our Father loves us so very much that instead of more suffering we do go through a purification process. It is a loving and educational process we go through that removes any stain we may have or any tendency toward sin no matter how small.

When we complete our purification process, we are then allowed to enter into God's heavenly kingdom with absolutely zero tendencies toward even the very smallest kinds of sin. We become pure and perfect and retain the essence of who we are meaning we retain every aspect of our personalities, our knowledge, and our interests and so on. One specific point Jesus made to me is we do not become robots in any way like the term pure and perfect may imply. We remain ourselves completely without even the smallest tendency to sin.

Booklet #1: CREATION

A Scientific View of Physical Creation's Destiny

The Entire Universe Is Connected

As a former NASA scientist, I am always amazed at the magnificent interlocking coherence between all the different variables that define the character and design of our physical universe. This is just one tiny example of what I mean. We all know that distance between two points is fixed unless one of them moves for some reason. Why? It is because God designed space to be extremely rigid.

There was a collision between two black holes 1.3 billion light years away from Earth. It took the gravity waves that this collision produced 1.3 billion years to get here, that collision produced $5 \times 10^{*47\text{th}}$ Joules of energy. The largest hydrogen bomb made on earth by the Russians called the Tsar Bomba produced $2 \times 10^{*17\text{th}}$ Joule's energy. That is $1 * 10^{30\text{th}}$ power less than the black hole collision. This is nothing more than a raindrop in a hurricane in comparison.

But the black hole collision was big enough to cause gravity waves across the whole universe. When the gravity waves reached earth, they affected the LIGO[10] gravitation instruments in the United States. Now, here is the fun part. Our Heavenly Father constructed our physical universe such that space and distance is extremely rigid. The black hole collision however did distort the space time continuum with gravity waves we detected. Our

---

[10] The Laser Interferometer Gravitational-Wave Observatory is a large-scale physics experiment and observatory designed to detect cosmic gravitational waves and to develop gravitational wave observations as an astronomical tool. Two large observatories were built in the United States with the aim of detecting gravitational waves by laser interferometry.

God's Grand Design

universe, its space, are so rigid the collision produced a distortion in our gravity instrumentation equivalent to the distance of 1 x 10 to the one-third power of the diameter of a single proton. The rigidness of the space time continuum is $1 * 10$ 20th power. This is enormously stiffer for then the best steel we can produce.

All this was designed into the construction and creation of the physical universe we live in. Lastly, this is just one itty-bitty example of the magnificent design characteristics of the physical realm we do call the universe.

Entropy Controls the Destiny of the Physical Universe

Entropy

Almighty God has designed our physical universe to have a finite existence just as he did our physical bodies each of us temporarily occupies. There is a scientific physical force that is built into the physical realm we call the universe. It applies to all things physical that are made of matter. The law of entropy, which is scientifically speaking the amount of chaos and randomness within a closed system, hard to believe because of its size, the physical universe is a closed system. It has specific dimensions we have not discovered yet scientifically.

This unstoppable trend toward randomness and chaos we experience every day of our lives but do not realize it. Now, please pardon me for I am experiencing a burst of nerd-ism or if you prefer geek-ism. I do have degrees in chemistry and physics. I even worked at NASA in my sophisticated lab full of advanced electronic analysis equipment that analyzed upper atmospheric particulate matter collected by the incredibly special extremely high altitude U2 spy planes. Spy planes our government used to spy on the Russians a number of decades ago.

The formula for entropy is: **$S = k \ln \Omega$**

Booklet #1: CREATION

S = Entropy
K = Boltzman's constant
Ω = number of micro states

Scientifically speaking, our universe was created initially with immeasurably low entropy. Ever since that microscopic moment in time 13.8 billion years ago the entire physical universe has been strongly trending toward increasing entropy. Mathematically speaking our universe will continue this process until there is nothing more than chaotic particles with no order or structures at all. The universe would become nothing more than a huge soup of random chaotic subatomic particles. That means entropy has reached its limit whatever that is.

This increasing entropy was clearly designed by our Creator heavenly Father. It is obvious he intended for the universe to have a limited lifespan. See, science can indeed give greater understanding to theological truths.

The closest to home is our own physical biological bodies. When we were young our bodies were working as intended by Our Heavenly Father. However, as time proceeds, we start to notice some things do not work as well as they used to. This is the law of entropy exercising its immutable self. This process of entropy or disintegration is built into the entire physical universe. The universe is not meant to be eternal. It has a fixed amount of time for its existence. Scientifically speaking if you take a radioactive substance it decays over time into a more stable substance. However, even that more stable substance will still decay on a longer timeline.

Basically, everything around us including our physical bodies is decaying toward unconnected physical particles. And they will not last forever either. So, everything physical has been planned to exist

God's Grand Design

for a finite time only. <u>However always keep in mind you are not, I repeat, not your physical body</u>. Evolutionists think we were self-assembled by random selection that resulted in our physical bodies. This is nothing more than complete satanic garbage.

The so-called evolutionists' theory is nothing more than a satanic lie. They try to make people believe all of us are nothing more than a pile of chemicals that accidentally came together through a process they call random selection. That term random selection is in and of itself an oxymoron. Said differently it contradicts itself. How can something be random yet at the same time be selective? The essence of every one of God's sacred children is they are given spiritual body that is eternal. We are spiritual beings, sacred children of Almighty God that came to earth to take the earth test which I have explained elsewhere. That is as long as you conduct your lives on earth according to the will of our loving Almighty Father.

The existing spiritual realm, as I said, is the largest realm of creation. However, all of Satan's demons and all of hell are subject to the forces of entropy or what Jesus likes to say the law of disintegration. Over some amount of time that I do not know about all of that will disintegrate back into nothingness from where it came.

Said differently, all the people that go to hell because of their earthly behaviors, they will slowly disintegrate back into nothingness from where they came. As that process occurs over an unknown amount of time, our memories of those sacred children of God will get weaker and weaker and weaker. It will be disintegration back into nothingness from where they came. There will come a time when memories of these people will not exist at all. How long this will take, I do not know. However, I do know this is precisely what will happen, and it is planned to happen by

Booklet #1: CREATION

Almighty God. Remember, the word nothingness means exactly that. A memory of those people who were in hell is something not nothing. Therefore, it must be concluded that even our memories of those people will also pass away into nothingness along with themselves.

God's Grand Design

The Heavenly Kingdom

My Constant Companions Jesus Christ and Mother Mary

My dear sacred children of Almighty God, the following information about the heavenly kingdom is the result of a conversation I had with Almighty God. Please remember that because I am God's Anointed Messenger, I have been given the gift of being able to speak with all three members of the Holy Trinity and our Blessed Mother Mary. This is a spiritual gift beyond anything I could have ever imagined.

Also please remember when Jesus Christ and our Blessed Mother Mary approached me a number of years ago. When they asking me to bring our Holy Father's message of love, peace, understanding and acceptance along with beautiful, advanced theology regarding God's creations. Jesus told me he and our Blessed Mother Mary will always be with me.

This is so beautiful! Because no matter where I am, or whom I am with, or what I am thinking or feeling, Jesus and Mary are always by my right side about eighteen inches away from my right shoulder. I cannot begin to express to you just how wonderful that is.

The questions below were answered by the Holy Trinity

Some Detailed Questions about the Heavenly Kingdom

With all of this in mind, I had a number of questions I would love to have Our Heavenly Father, Jesus Christ, The Holy Spirit give us further knowledge about. The following section on my questions to our Lord and Savior Jesus Christ is my best effort to explore deep information about God's creation both seen and unseen.

Booklet #1: CREATION

Almighty God Answers:

Question 1. Has the Heavenly realm been in existence for eternity like the Holy Trinity?

July 30, 2022
5:28 PM

"My dear children - the Trinity has always lived in the Heavenly realm. It has no beginning; it exists now and will live on. It is eternal where what you call time in the physical realm does not exist. Heaven is all around you whether you realize it or not. Heaven is also a place. Within this realm there are different forms of life. Forms that exist, of course us within the Trinity, Almighty God our Father, me (Jesus Christ), and the Holy Spirit which proceeds from us within the Trinity outward to the other realms of existence.

Question 2

What are some details of the Heavenly realm, describe the realm of Almighty God?

Heavenly Details

Yet, it is true. You asked about defining in more detail what the Heavenly realm is like. It is not like the physical realm or in the spiritual realm you currently reside in.

1. *It is laws of physics for example that are very much different than those on earth within the physical realm. It is a paradise for all of God's sacred children that qualify through their behavior demonstrated during their earthly existence. Jesus Christ told me on several occasions that it is a paradise we can barely imagine.*

2. There is far more freedom. To come and go as you wish without any effort on your part. All you need to do is think about where you want to be, and you may will it for you to be there.

3. All communications within our sacred children and the Angels and of course us within the Trinity are as you would call telepathic. That is not to say there is no sound in the Heavenly realm, it is quite the opposite. Your Lord Father in Heaven loves to hear the angels sing and he loves to hear the voices of his children such as yourself. If you cannot sing on earth, that is certainly not a problem for you will be surprised at how deliciously wonderful you will sound in the Heavenly realm.

4. Angels will come and go and be with you as your constant companion if you wish.

5. All of you will know each other and their histories of each other and their struggles on earth if that is what you wish. The depth of love you will feel within the Heavenly realm is far more intense and pleasurable than you can imagine.

6. One of the aspects of the heavenly kingdom is we as God's sacred children will again be able to think things into existence. We will be able to think of where we would like to go and then will that to happen and it will happen.

7. We will have instant access to all of our friends we knew before we went to earth and the friends we made while taking the earth test.

Booklet #1: CREATION

> **8. We will be surrounded with a magnificent atmosphere of pure love. Gone completely are all remnants of the rampant negativity on earth.**
>
> **9. Any memories of evil on earth will quickly fade into the distant past and will have zero effect on us.**
>
> **10.   Each of us after we enter the heavenly kingdom will go through a purification process. This will be a delightful thing because it will be the shedding of residual bad memories and anything remotely no matter how small connected to Satan. The entire Trinity and our Blessed Mother Mary are perfect and pure. And so, we will be also.**

My son, I know you remember the golden orb that appeared to you on the jet halfway across the Pacific Ocean. That is when you were told the following words, "God loves you." Along with that simple message came a magnificently intense feeling of love for you. I know you felt like running up and down the aisle of the jet proclaiming God loves us. It is good you chose not to for that would have created such an incident of confusion among the other people that it would not be good for them. [11]

---

[11] This spiritual experience was completely unexpected. I was flying to Manila in the Philippines by myself and suddenly I saw the most beautiful golden basketball sized orb that was emitting the most beautiful rays of golden light. After the first 20 seconds of looking at this gorgeous site, it said to me, "God loves you!" It stayed over the aisle between the seats about one row ahead of me, but I could see it ever so clearly. What it said to me was magnificent and I could feel the intense love that the Golden orb was transmitting to me. While it was emitting this beautiful love to me, I was amazed that no one else close to me on the jet noticed anything. It was only me that could see the orb and feel the intense love that it showed me. After a time, way too short for me, it started to fade away and then I noticed that I was not hearing any of the normal jet sounds while it was there. It was only after the orb left that the sounds of the jet returned. This is one of the most magnificent spiritual experiences I have had in my life.

As I said earlier on the realms of existence are contained within the Heavenly realm. But this does not mean in any way things cannot flow into and out from the Heavenly realm without strong conditions and protection from Satan and his demons. The Heavenly realm with all its different physics and roles of spirituality is completely fortified from any intrusion from those spirits that do not belong there no matter how small the intrusion might be.

Within the Heavenly realm there are different layers of existence. There are seven layers to be exact. Each of the ascending layers, become filled with more and more gratification, fulfillment, intensifying love. And other rewards that are consistent with what each of our children has shown themselves to be while they are on the earth.

Question 3
What are the sizes of the different realms?

Size is really a very relativistic thing within all of God's creation. There are no absolute dimensions at all. However, much too many people are surprised the heavenly kingdom is not the largest realm. But if you are in the heavenly kingdom, it is infinite in all directions. Jesus Christ himself told me this some time ago.

The spiritual realm is the largest one. It must accommodate uncountable spiritual beings such as angels, such as the spiritual part of you and me. It also is home for hell, Satan, and his demons. This is why Satan has access to our minds. It is because our minds reside within the spiritual realm. This gives us access, direct access to Our Heavenly Father, to our Lord and Savior Jesus Christ, to the Holy Spirit that proceeds from them and to our Blessed Mother Mary. But it also gives Satan access to our individual minds.

Booklet #1: CREATION

It is for this reason both the sacred and the evil have access to each of our minds. This is why we are tempted by satanic forces, and we must use Our Heavenly gifts of behavioral expectations from our loving Father. If we give into Satan and whatever temptations he is offering, this leads directly to hell. Therefore, it is accurate to say our individual minds are a battlefield between the heavenly love /good and the satanically evil.

Size wise which is something our children can relate to, Heaven has no outer boundaries and within it, it contains all the other spiritual realms you have described within this magnificent book.[12] As you know my son, we within the Trinity are pure spiritual beings that encompass the entire realm of what you call Heaven. Again, it is infinite in all of the multiple dimensions your scientists are working on, and it contains all the different time dimensions as well.

It is exceedingly easy for us within the Trinity to use all these different dimensions of space, time. And other aspects of dimensionality to serve us in the Trinity to explore an infinite different variety of attributes, qualities, intense love from each of us in the Trinity back to the others.

Within your book dear son, you are exploring the characteristics and nature of the physical realm, the spiritual realm and now the Heavenly realm. There are other realms but none of those pertain to your existence within our divine goals for you, our children. We within the Trinity are easily able to create more dimensions and more realms of existence if we so choose and that serve our purpose.

Remember all that is needed is a thought to bring something into existence and it is done. What you call Heaven has been our

---

[12] Jesus is referring to the master book of all the booklets. "God's Grand Design Of All Creation For Your Redemption"

home from before eternity began. I know to you that may sound like an oxymoron, but it is not. Considering all the different dimensions we have created you are unaware of, that statement is not understandable.

Remember my son that the creation of the physical realm and the spiritual realm is matched perfectly with the design of your human body. This is so the needs of your physical body are met with the resources available to you on earth. And as I said before, it is your brain and the overlying spiritual body you have that is completely in tune with the spiritual realm.

Many people have speculated on the size of the Holy Kingdom where God Almighty resides and where the Holy Spirit and I call home. All of our creations are from Our Heavenly realm. Your Father so loves his children that not only after you were thought into existence, considering how individually differ, you lived with your Father in Heaven as spiritual beings for a long time. This is so he could enjoy each of you personally. And love you in the ways that match your talents, your attributes, your characteristics and what's been decided would be the trajectory of your life once you are born on earth.

What your Biblical literature says about the details of which God knows each of you when it says Almighty God even knows the number of hairs on your head, this is so true. For Almighty God, resides not only in around and through all of creation but we also know every detail of your life, your motivations, and everything you say and do. For it is in this way we are able to separate the sheep from the goats. There are no secrets within all of creation.
[13]

---

[13] This is an amazing statement by Jesus. Yes, there are no secrets within the spiritual realm which includes heaven. Everything and I do mean everything is visible and known by everyone else. It always amazes me what

Booklet #1: CREATION

The size of the Heavenly Kingdom is on purpose smaller than what I described Heaven to be. For the Heavenly Kingdom where we in the Trinity reside necessarily is smaller. Yet for our children that join us within the Heavenly realm eternally, it will seem unending in every way. There will be no restrictions upon the children of God. Yet at the same time there will be some responsibilities for each of our sacred children. However, this is a very light load for the Heavenly realm is meant to be a paradise for all of our Father's children.

Our children will have all of creation at their feet to explore and be in wonderment of what their Heavenly Father created for them. Remember, all creation you see in the Heavens above and this bears within you and other things are specifically designed to create a pathway from the wreckage in your minds. This wreckage caused by Lucifer now known as Satan and all of his demons.

If there is, as some of your poets have said, a key to the gates of Heaven is simply stated as <u>belief and faith in me as your Lord and Savior. And love in your hearts for all your fellow children of God</u>.

Question 4

How are Heaven's borders protected from evil, from Satan and his demons? And is there truly only one entrance, or gate, that allows entry into the Heavenly realm?

---

people think, the dishonest and cruel people think that they can hide what they do. They cannot. They will have such a surprised look on their faces when they have to face our Lord and Savior Jesus Christ shortly after they leave this world. They will be confronted with every rotten thing they said, every rotten thing they did and every motivation they had to do all the damage they did while on the earth.

Jesus Christ
January 5, 2024

You asked about how the Kingdom of God in Heaven is protected from those who do not belong. There are a number of ways that this is accomplished but you will not understand them. But one way you will is the many very powerful angels we have that are able to keep things well in order based on the will of your Father.

Is there one gate to the entrance of Heaven? Yes, my son there is one path to the Heavenly realm and there is one gate and one gate only. Only those found in the book of life and have kept the word of your Father in Heaven, love others of his children as you love yourself and the commandments given by God to Moses.

It is only those that find their names in the sacred book. And as you and I have discussed before, only the few will find their names written in this book of life. There are many more things I could tell you, my dear son. But I believe this will answer your questions. And the understandings of the nature of existence by all of your readers who decides to take the time and effort to read the words. Words contained in this magnificent book you have written with of course the help we give you from the Trinity.

I love you my dear son."

Question 5

Just how many make it back to the Heavenly Kingdom?

My dear Lord and Savior, recently I watched a video on YouTube quoting a number of well-known clergy, bishops and so on of the Catholic Church. They said those living in mid-evil times, a terribly few number of God sacred children would be qualified to live within the holy kingdom of heaven after they passed away. This bothered me greatly because the percentage of people is never more

Booklet #1: CREATION

than 1% or 2%. My dearest loving Lord and Savior I know we discussed this point before, and you told me it was more like 30%. Can you please give me more detailed enlightenment on this question? Thank you, dear Lord.

Yes, my dearest son, I know that video bothered you immensely. It is because you love so much the others of God sacred children and to think that almost all are going to hell is very painful for you.

The answer you are seeking is when you take the entire world's population into account it is what I previously told you approximately 30%. But if we were to break that down into different pieces, it would be something like this:

Christians: approximately 60% only. This is because a lot of people that call themselves Christians really do not practice Christianity in their daily lives therefore more secular and ignore the beauty of Christianity.

Muslims: This is where things get tough. If a person is born a Muslim, the only worldview they are taught is one 0 of dominion and hatred. They are taught women are second-class citizens. They are taught to kill and kill again. This however does not mean all Muslims go to hell. Many Muslims use their built-in sense of love for other human beings which was built into them before they were born. Many Muslims follow their instincts and reject what their leaders tell them, but they have to do this silently. You have said many times Islam is a manifestation of Satan on earth. You hit the nail on the head my dear son. Islam thrives on hatred and fear. This is built into Muslim societies. Basically, it is that they believe in the false god Allah that they tell you to believe in or they will kill you. This is both pure hatred and pure fear. This is exactly how Satan rules his kingdom.

Their ultimate goal is to control the entire world and dominate everyone in it which is exactly the opposite of what your Heavenly Father wants. This in and of itself is the highest form of Satanic action.

So, my dear son the percentage across all Muslim peoples that go to heaven is quite small. It is approximately 7% only. No more.

If it were bunched together, the rest of the different religions on earth the percentage of those people who love Almighty God and love their neighbors and are forgiving toward others, it is approximately 23%. Too many of them worship false gods even though on the surface they are good people by secular measurements. Please write down for your readers the summary you so expertly created to summarize how to get to heaven.

(A New Booklet is coming in a number of months that has the title, "Getting into Heaven.")

This is all that should be said for now. Your question is very hard-hitting and drills down to the exact truth of things on earth. I know all of your activities are aimed at increasing the numbers of God sacred children that will qualify to enter the gates of the kingdom of heaven. I deeply thank you for that.

One follow-on question, my dearest Lord: why the percentage is so low from these esteemed leaders of the Catholic Church. I think it may be because of church history and during the times in the ancient past these numbers were given is when the Catholic Church had not grown so much yet.

My dear son, you indeed are a very perceptive person and yes you are close to the truth. The number of people that make it into the

Booklet #1: CREATION

heavenly kingdom is a flexible number across time. As an example, the numbers I have given you are what are current and based on the existence of Christian churches that preach the real Christian Bible and teachings. They teach what it is you understand as fundamental Christianity. During the ancient time when the leaders of the church were on earth what they said was somewhat pessimistic but close to the truth at that time.

Since then, the church has grown enormously and its effect on the world's population has been very favorable for making people qualify to enter the kingdom. And as I just said it has grown to about 30% now.

A Follow-On Question:

First, dear Lord Jesus, I want to repeat what you already know, just how much I love you and everything you do for not only me but for all of God's sacred children. Thank you, dear Lord Jesus.

Now, since talking about different groups of people and how many make it back into the heavenly kingdom, it occurs to me politics does indeed enter into everything we do in our lives. It is inescapable to be strongly influenced by Democrat versus Republican in our beloved United States of America. Split the country's population into the two groups of liberal versus conservative or stated differently Democrat versus Republican, knowing the foundational values of each party are diametrically opposed. What would be the percentages of each party that make it back into the heavenly kingdom?

Oh boy my dear son, this is a deeply penetrating question. First, as you know like in all other groupings, there are many good people in both parties. But dear son you are correct that the foundational theology or lack of it is vastly different for Democrats versus Republicans. Democrats have created a façade of caring for the disadvantaged and packed the blame on Republicans when in fact they use this skillfully to gain more and more central power in your government. The Republicans on the other hand honor the principles and morality of what your country was created on. These values are indeed based on Judeo Christian ethics and morality. The United States is the only country in the world that has biblical foundations. I'm sure you know this is why the United States has been increasingly attacked by other atheist and communist nations.

Now, regard the political divisions in the United States. The Democrat foundational values centers upon the "self", meaning each person is more important than any other person especially who they consider their enemies which are those in the Republican Party. This sets up a pattern of hatred. It is, "if you do not believe as I do, you are my enemy". This thought process is of Satan.

Additionally, the Democrat party is filled with people that purposely do not work because they know they can get money from others of God's sacred children that do work honestly for their families. It is a very vicious system of slavery and purposeful parasites that feed off of the earnings of those who do their best to work hard. My dear son you know the origin of this thought is Satan himself. To the extent people fall for this satanic deception and view God's children as their enemies, necessarily the percentage of Democrats in your country that make it back into Our Heavenly kingdom is quite low.

From those children of God deciding to work hard for them and family and follow the three rules of existence on earth as so eloquently described, they will make it back to the heavenly kingdom. It makes me cry thinking about all those others who believe the satanic lie of the Democrat party and want to live off what others earn, these people will not make it back to heaven.

Booklet #1: CREATION

You asked what the percentages of each are. Sadly, those who call themselves Democrats, only 23% make it back into the heavenly kingdom. The rest have swallowed the satanic lies as distributed by your Democrat party. This is because they support the ugly sin of abortion, the murder of innocent sacred children of your Father. Parasite type behavior is promoted by the Democrat party and the conscious and willful rhetoric of pitting groups of your Almighty Father's sacred children against others of his sacred children. This is pure satanic thought.

The Republican Party is much better than this. For those who call themselves Republicans a far higher percentage are those who work hard to provide for their families and do not expect a free ride from others of God sacred children. They are far more apt to also follow all three of the major behavioral rules as laid down by our Father and described in a simple manner by you my dear son. The number I'm going to give you will surprise you greatly but as you know it will be complete truth. The percentage of Republicans that make it back into the heavenly kingdom is 78%.

I hope this answers your question my dear son I love you more than you know.

As another note my dear son you already know you are entering into the end times as prophesized by your Blessed Mother Mary back in 1917. Thank you for doing a complete book on all of this and allowing your Blessed Mother to speak freely with your commitment to publish every word she says. The Catholic Church I founded has been serving itself and not my sacred children.

(Authors note: this book will appear as a booklet. Its title will be :)

"God's Grand Design"

Booklet 2,

Our Blessed Mother Mary, In Her Words"

Question 6:

What happened to the people on earth that lived before you were born as our Lord and Savior? They had no knowledge. I think I know what you are going to say but I would love to hear it from you my dear Lord.

January 7, 2024
Jesus Christ

Your Father in heaven is very merciful and fair. It would be very much unfair to his sacred children born before I was to earth. They were given a special place in heaven where they could choose to return to earth to take the Earth test like everyone else. Or they could choose to not return to earth for the Earth test again and be among those who made the same choice of remaining in the heavenly kingdom. All of these people that were born before me were treated with God's loving kindness and given the choice I just described.

This is about as much detail as I wish to get into now my dear son. For if we were to go further in this line of questions my answers would become somewhat not understandable due to the complexity of the different situations on earth.

The bottom line is your loving Father in heaven as you know gives everyone the maximum possibility of entering the kingdom according to his standards of behavior. We know each and every one of his sacred children that were born to earth before me. It is easy for us to tell which ones deserve entry into the kingdom in which ones do not. They will be judged by the same standards as everyone is with the understanding they did not know anything about me and given leeway for that reason. All of this is on an individual basis just like it is today.

I love you my dear son,
Jesus Christ, your Lord, and Savior who you loves so very much.

Booklet #1: CREATION

Question 7:

Once God's sacred children return to the heavenly kingdom, is there any chance that some could fall out of the kingdom due to violation or something of the rules of existence?

Jesus Christ
1/15/2024

No, my dear son, those who enter the heavenly kingdom are pure and perfect. Do not misinterpret the last phrase pure and perfect. That does not mean somehow those who are allowed to enter the heavenly kingdom somehow are changed to something different than which they are. They remain as themselves without the slightest inkling toward anything negative in any way.

Upon the death of a believer in your Heavenly Father, all will go through a purification process to remove all the little bits of damage from living on a satanic planet. This is such an exciting and loving experience for all those preparing to enter into the heavenly kingdom. Although my dear son, since your sins are few this entrance process will be joyful for you.

I know you continue to grieve for the woman you knew ever so well and tried to help. That moment when she was screaming after she died, and I asked you to help her, you did the right thing and you saw me take her hand and lead her into the heavenly realm. She did not enter the kingdom because she needed a lot of emotional and psychological help to overcome the damage her mother did to her. As I told you before, she was what we call an edge case where if she put enough effort into changing herself for the better, she would be in heaven today. As you know your Father and I did everything we could. Your Father is so loving he wants all of his children to be able to return to the kingdom. We made all possible efforts to help your close friend, but it was her freewill choice to leave the kingdom because she could not see herself behaving the way she needed to in the kingdom. This hardly happens at all, but she chose to not continue her therapy and through her free will choice she was kindly and gently let out of the heavenly realm.

So, my dearest son, this is an excellent question and very perceptive. I can summarize by saying, once you are in the heavenly kingdom, you are in for all eternity with no possibility of leaving heaven.

Question 8:

Note: This section normally belongs in the coming booklet titled, "Getting into Heaven." But I feel covering this now is a good thing. As Heaven, Earth, and God's sacred children are the focus of everything Our Heavenly Loving Father, you dear Lord and Savior and our Holy Spirit that proceeds from you have done for all of us.

Before all of us sacred children came to earth for our "earth test," did we know how awful earth is? What are the other details of our knowledge of earth before coming here? What is the earth test preparation process like?

Jesus Christ
January 19, 2024

Oh, my dear son, thank you so very much for asking this question. This will be very enlightening for all of your Father's sacred children on earth. To begin, the preparation process is actually quite extensive. Your Father does not want any of his sacred children to go into a situation they did not know about beforehand and approved of what will happen. As you know, your Heavenly Father is ever so merciful and fair in everything. This includes the preparation for going to earth. Here is a list of the items that are covered in detail:

Booklet #1: CREATION

Everyone is informed dishonesty and lies permeate the entire earthly realm. This is something that surprises all sacred children because their entire existence was within the perfect and pure environment where any lies or deceptions are impossible. This is one of the biggest items they have to get used to.

Another item is they will understand their existence on earth is quite short actually. The average lifespan is anywhere between 50 years to 90 years old and not much more for a few of the sacred children.

They will be told about violence on earth and wars. This shocks many sacred children and upon learning this, Our Father is not disappointed at all if they decide to change their mind and stay within the heavenly realm. This is certainly not a blemish in any way.

They are told life is quite difficult to provide the necessary resources for themselves and their family. In heaven just a thought will bring food but in heaven that is not a necessity in any way. It is more of an optional delight. Your dear wife, Marilyn, when she finished her preparation to enter the kingdom, she ate a lot of food because during those five years fighting cancer food tasted like cardboard to her. And so she wanted to feast upon all the delicacies she could think of. This also was extra glorious for her because she knew she would not gain weight like she fought against during earthly existence.

Everyone learns about the necessity to work to provide food, shelter, and clothing. This was completely alien to God's sacred children.

When you visited your first granddaughter while she was preparing to come to earth, she was at the point where she was preparing for her life theme that everyone must be educated for. This varies from child to child depending on what their goals are.

These goals are typically what you would call spiritual self enhancement. Like you my dear son, you told your Father your life theme was to put other people ahead of yourself. That is a particularly hard path in the physical realm with Satan always lurking about. On this you have done wonderfully.

This preparation process is conducted by loving intelligent angels that answer all of God's sacred children's questions. It is individual tutorials that take place, and they are in detail based upon where on earth the child wants to be born, the individual man and woman of their choice and other minor details. All of this is discussed to ensure the proper foundational elements are present so God's sacred child can live up the opportunity of learning more about creation and their heavenly Father in a different way.

Of all the sacred children in heaven there are not that many that choose to come to earth. You could say the children that come to earth are of the adventurous type wanting to take in all the information of more and more of God's creations. If they come back to the heavenly kingdom, they will have achieved great and wondrous knowledge, joy and be able to give tutorials to others of God's children who decided to remain in the kingdom. Their lives will be enriched tremendously, and they will end up being closer to their Father than they ever thought possible for they have successfully rejected Satan in all aspects of their earthly lives.

Question 9:

What percentage of the sacred children in the Heavenly Kingdom decided to stay vs. come to earth?

My dear son, I know you like statistics and science and you are very good at that so it is no surprise you would ask this question in terms of percentages. I would say to you that the percentages of all of God sacred children that decide to come and take the earthly

Booklet #1: CREATION

test is relatively small. When someone wants to take the earth test the analogy would be like the astronauts that went to the moon. Not many people became astronauts, test pilots and other adventurous ones that took on those tasks for the betterment of all others of God sacred children. Everyone was so proud of each earth test sacred child, and they wish him ever so well and they do monitor the earth test sacred children and their progress to their lives. It is risky for sure, and everyone knows that before they come to earth. Those that succeed will reap rich rewards for doing so and have demonstrated to the entire spiritual realm and heavenly realm they indeed love their Almighty Father so very much.

Question 10:

How long does the preparation for earth take?

This preparation process can really not be measured in terms of earthly time. Remember there is no time in the heavenly realm where the preparations take place. Suffice to say it is very thorough and complete before each sacred child is born to the earth.

Question 11:

To someone already in the Kingdom, what is to be gained by taking a statistical serious risk of hell by coming to earth? That tells me somehow these sacred children really did not know themselves as they thought they did. Is that correct dear Lord? Something is missing in my understanding of things.

This is an excellent question. There is always room for personal spiritual growth within each and every sacred child of your Father. So many people think that coming to heaven is the end of the road, like you have made it and after that things stay static. Nothing could be further from the truth. Your loving Father encourages all of his sacred children to learn and develop deeper and deeper into their ability to love and to know all about the spiritual realm and its opportunities for personal growth. Remember, there are seven levels in heavenly existence. Each level represents higher and higher spiritual growth and development. Along with rising higher in the heavenly realm come greater and greater rewards of knowledge, depth of experienced love and fulfillment for all those who grow personally. Actually, there is no end to this and along each step of the way you become closer and closer to the Trinity.

As I know you so very well dear son, after you return to heaven, I know you will continue your pursuits of personal spiritual growth and knowledge. As they say within your business world on earth, you are upwardly mobile. I hope my response is fulfilling enough that it answers the depth of your questions which are all excellent. All the people who read your written materials and listen to your presentations will be far better off spiritually and will understand the entire message of what your Heavenly Father created, and you are delivering. Thank you, my dear son thank you so very much.

A Related Story

Regarding the preparation work before coming to earth, I remember being allowed to see my first grandchild as she was preparing to come to earth. Instantly we knew each other. I still can see what she looked like, a white bowling pin with two dark eyes and a round black nose. I also saw many others soon to be born bowling pins walking around doing their business preparing. We looked at each other but did not say anything. I did not know what to say, frankly. It was a quiet place to be in.

Booklet #1: CREATION

Question 12:

My dear Lord and Savior Jesus, I understand completely every sacred child of our loving Father in heaven is "perfect and pure" and they have no inclination whatsoever to sin in any way. However, when a sacred child chooses to be born on earth to take the earth test, most will reject Our Heavenly Father and end up in hell. This tells me that deep within them, deep within their spiritual being lays a potentiality to reject Our Heavenly Father even though they are perfect and pure and live in heaven. Additionally in other sections we have shared together you mentioned everyone in heaven does not have the slightest inkling toward sin.

How can that be? What is it I am missing or not understanding?

January 9, 2024
Jesus Christ

Boy…is that ever a good question. Everything you understand my dear son is perfectly correct. Every sacred child of God that comes to take the earth test is indeed perfect and pure otherwise they would not be in the heavenly kingdom. The information that is additional and what you need to answer this is all of God sacred children need to understand there are different levels of strength within their status of perfect and pure. Some sacred children are far stronger than others even though both certainly fit within the category of perfect and pure.

It is like a tree in a hurricane. Satan is the hurricane on earth. The different trees exposed to the hurricane are that some remain upright, and others are blown down. It depends on the strength of the tree. This analogy applies to all of God sacred children who are in heaven. Each sacred child does not know just how strong they are in standing up to satanic pressures and temptations. That is a deeply individual component of their spiritual being.

God's Grand Design

It is true God's sacred children are unable to examine themselves down to the last particle of their existence. The situation is dynamic when God's children come to earth. What I mean by this is. Many times the weak sacred children exposed to the dishonesty and violence of the earthly realm, they see this firsthand, and will rebel forcefully against Satan and his rejection of their loving Almighty Father. Being exposed to evil is so repugnant to the sacred children they literally steel up their strength in their rejection of Satan and everything he stands for.

I know you remember the moment in time when you were a young teenager living at your parent's house on Inverness way. Your Father was exceptionally cruel to you that day resulting in your crying, and you hugged him. He was so cold and loveless toward you while you were hugging him you told yourself silently these words, "I will never treat my children the way you treat me."

That incident increased your rejection of everything Satan does in the earthly realm in the behaviors of people that have given themselves over to satanic rejection of your loving Father. In that moment in time, you became a Christian warrior who loves Almighty God more than you ever did in your past. You experienced for the first time how ugly and destructive satanic people are like your Father. No longer did you try to please him in any way. You gained great strength in that short moment in time. And you saw your Father for what he really was. You were repulsed as you should be.

Others of God sacred children give in to the temptations of Satan. They were pure and perfect when they left the heavenly kingdom. But for a whole potpourri of reasons, they could not withstand the satanic lures of lies, deceit and sinful attractions.

Booklet #1: CREATION

I hope my dearest of sons this answers your question not only for you but for everyone who reads this magnificent work you are doing on their behalf.

Question 13:

For the sake of all of our Father's sacred children who read this, I would like to get into the details of the rewards of those who make it back into the heavenly kingdom. I know their love for God increases greatly, and they become much closer to the divine source of all creation. They know themselves much better than they ever did while in the kingdom. Many times, they become far stronger as spiritual human beings who love you. Beyond this my dear Lord Jesus, I know there are other glorious things that happen, and I would like to understand more of these details.

Jesus Christ
January 20, 2024

Oh, my dear son, this is a wonderful question, and it penetrates right into the truth of all of God sacred children. As I said before, it is a minority of sacred children in the kingdom that elect to go back to take the earth test. So, your question is very appropriate. Everybody thinks the heavenly kingdom is the end goal and there is nothing beyond that. This is certainly true in a sense. But the heavenly kingdom in and of itself offers an eternity of personal spiritual growth. It is not stagnant as many people assume it to be. It is a very dynamic paradise as I have explained before.

Remember dear son all of God sacred children always retain their beautiful gift of free choice or free will. Even in the heavenly kingdom. All of our sacred children are encouraged but never forced to expand their ability to love, to cherish and to increase their knowledge of who they are and where they are. They may choose not to do these things, which is perfectly acceptable by the

Trinity. But in doing the things that resulted in the expansion of their spiritual being will result in many rewards. Returning to earth and to take the earth test is a very strong indicator they wish to grow far beyond what they were before they went to earth.

It is on earth the battle between your Heavenly Father and Satan is demonstrated every moment of every day. This is great knowledge to have, and it educates others of God sacred children remaining in the heavenly kingdom. This is because those who are in the kingdom have the ability to observe everything that goes on during their brothers and sisters taking the earth test. They can see the progress of those who are on earth.

Once a heavenly sacred child completes the earth test, they all will be damaged to some degree or another. They will be damaged by exposure to satanic sin just by rubbing shoulders with those who have given themselves to Satan in one way or another. So, in summary,

1. *Our sacred children will expand their knowledge and strength toward the heavenly realm and understand more fully the utter ugliness and destructive of sinful behavior.*

2. *In your case my dear son Satan visited you himself on three separate occasions where he threatened you on each occasion three times yelling at you, "I will get you!" Now you know Satan personally and know him very well and you completely reject every smallest particle of what he says or does.*

3. *To God's other sacred children remaining in the heavenly kingdom, the return to the kingdom of God's sacred children successfully endured the earth test; they will be greeted by celebrations like a returning warrior. This is*

Booklet #1: CREATION

> *because that is exactly what the earth test is...a battle against Satan. In the process our sacred children learn so much about themselves and what they want to do upon their return to heaven.*
>
> 4. *Those who return will certainly receive a higher level within the kingdom that allows them to experience greater feelings of love, of fulfillment and being closer to the three of us in the Trinity. It will be much like the experience you had when the golden orb appeared to you on the jet halfway across the Pacific Ocean. Your entire body tingled I know and for those who return to the heavenly kingdom, those kinds of experiences will increase greatly for them. They will experience the bodily tingling of love much like what you did when you were administering Reiki healing to your wife Marilyn before she returned to us.*

So, my dearest son, your success in navigating the earth test results in not only benefiting you personally but also our sacred children who observe your progress on earth. They learn from your experiences as well as you do. I hope this answers your question to the detail you had in mind.

Question 14:

Where Will I be?

Jesus Christ
January 22, 2024

This is a very good question. If someone follows the three fundamental rules of existence on earth for all of God's sacred children, all of us will be in heaven with our Father in paradise described earlier. If anybody does not follow the behavior rules of our Father, this means for sure they have rejected Almighty God in their life. And the very clear conclusion regarding their fitness for heaven is they will not fit into the heavenly kingdom. They have proven that by rejecting our loving Father's rules for our existence.

I will get into this subject in detail in one of my next booklets. It will probably be titled "Getting into Heaven."

I must mention at this point there is no excuse for bad behavior while we are all on earth. Every single one of Our Heavenly Father's sacred children are born with a basic understanding of right versus wrong. If you look at the behavior of little babies and observe closely, you will see they believe everything you tell them. If someone takes a toy from them, they will cry because inwardly they know that an infraction of God's rules has been committed against them. However, the older they get the more used to earthly behaviors (satanic) is understood.

As your author and Anointed Messenger of Our Heavenly Father, I love you so very much and I hope this booklet brings you closer to the Holy Trinity and Blessed Mother Mary.

Blessings and Love to All!

Richard

Booklet #1: CREATION

Appendix 1

One Example of Our Holy Father Speaking To Me

File Name: Father Speaks About the Book and NRB

This bolded italic text below is a message from Our Heavenly Father spoken to me when I was in a jet halfway across the Pacific Ocean going from San Francisco to Manila. This happened December 3, 2023. I ask you to seriously consider how is it our Father in heaven knew exactly where I was. He always does!

Like all my communications with Our Heavenly Father, he speaks to me into the spiritual part of my mind. He speaks in English and speaks slowly so I can transcribe everything he says into ultimately a Microsoft Word text file.

The first part of what he said addressed the fact Satan was attacking me just a few minutes before he came and started speaking to me. There are certain things he wants done related to the book "God's Grand Design of All Creation for Your Redemption." I followed His wishes!

My Dear Son,

That was Satan; he wants to scare you as much as he can. He does not understand your intense love and how much of a fighter you are. My love for you is infinite. For this I thank you enormously. The loving effect you will have on my children on earth is enormous.

My dear son, as my son told you, things will start to happen and it will be good, it will be very good you go to the meeting called NRB. You will meet certain people there that will be enormously helpful to make your book, my book known to so many people that will love you and embrace you.

And as you know because you are so intelligent, this is as you would say stir the pot of the satanic crowd. This will be hard for you, but I know you will do well. Go to Tennessee and meet as many people as you can. Give them the book. I prefer you give them the original version. Your publisher has every good intention in changing the title. But it is my will the first book you created is the one that will succeed.

Go with that one my dearest son. So, I will be with you every second of every day. Speak freely in your own way the truth is that I have given you. I will guide you and Jesus your Savior will guide you and be with you every moment of every day. You have my highest of blessings. I love you my dearest son.

And yes, I want you to use your true title: My anointed messenger.

Thank you, I love you.

Booklet #1: CREATION

Appendix 2

Who Is Your Author, Richard Ferguson?

This is an amazingly simple yet extremely hard question for me to answer. This is because it contains my Divine Title that you have never heard before about any singular human being on the earth. I have struggled for a long time of how to introduce myself to all others of God's sacred children. The master book, "God's Grand Design of All Creation for Your Redemption" was released to the public in April or May earlier this year 2023. It contains my divine title.

In my prayers to Our Heavenly Father, I asked what I should do. His response is consistently the same, *"**my dearest son, just tell my sacred children who you really are and the title I have given you.**"* (Yes, Father always addresses me as His dearest son.) My title our Father has given me is:

"Our Father's Anointed Messenger"

I am an Anointed Messenger from God. Our Father has asked me to bring to all His sacred children His message of, *"**love, understanding, acceptance and especially advanced theology of His creations**.* This includes how all His sacred children fit into His grand plan for our salvation.

But please know I have a very intimate and loving relationship with the three persons of the Trinity and our Blessed Mother Mary. And yes, without any doubt I can speak with each one personally and separately. If I asked a question, they would answer me immediately without error for they are perfect and pure in every way. I speak with Jesus at least a dozen times each day of my life. Our Father in Heaven has told me to always use my given title. I am aptly called, "His Anointed Messenger." I am this one and only

God's Grand Design

Anointed Messenger because of what I said to Our Heavenly Father before I was born on this earth. There are particularly good reasons I have that title.

The story of how I received this title from Our Heavenly Father is a long one that reaches back into my history before I was born to this earth. I might include this story in a future writing I will do.

Both Jesus and Mary are my constant companions every minute of every day and they know my thoughts and my feelings about things where I do not even have to express them. They already know because they are so intimately close to me.

I was not always God's anointed messenger. This revelation occurred a number of years ago much to my personal surprise. Our Heavenly Father asked me to be his anointed messenger to all his sacred children on earth and to author a book that contained his personal message to all his sacred children. I answered yes, I will. I did not have any clear idea about what I said yes to. But I knew through my love of God and faith that whatever it would be is something incredibly good. So, I said yes.

Also, I have a binding covenant with Our Heavenly Father that is simple but immensely powerful. The covenant is "I will always tell the truth in everything I say." I will never lie so as to mislead others of God's sacred children. To me, telling a lie is a grievous, painful, and horrific sin against my loving heavenly Father. I just cannot imagine telling even the smallest lie. This booklet is completely true with every word, every sentence, and every thought.

I Will Make the Biography Stuff Short As Possible

Academically I went to get bachelor's degrees in chemistry and physics, minors in philosophy and theology. A master's degree in business and then later in my life I answered the call from Almighty God and earned a master's degree in pastoral ministry in

Booklet #1: CREATION

spirituality and theology. The tug of Almighty God I felt was extraordinarily strong inside me and I wrote six spiritual books before I wrote, "God's Grand Design of All Creation for Your Redemption."

Along the way during my life, I got my commercial pilot's license along with instrument rating and flight instructor rating. I actually feel safer in the air than on the ground as long as I am the pilot. Go figure. Needing to ensure a solid financial future for my family, I also got a real estate broker's license.

Over the course of my life, I have experienced many spiritual encounters of various kinds. For some reason, Our Heavenly Father wanted me to experience these things such as, seeing my first granddaughter in the heavenly realm before she was born to earth. When my late wife of 38 years contracted terminal cancer, I was shown exactly what would happen and when. When I bitterly complained to God about this that she would die in five years I was swept out of my body and into the heavenly realm and I spoke with two Heavenly elders. That did not change anything, but I felt better at least that the heavenly heard what I had to say.

Satan knows me and my earthly mission. As a result, when I was in my mid thirty's, He viciously attacked me on three separate occasions. All three were in the middle of the night; all were horrifying like nothing people experience or could understand. Yes, Satan really does exist and my encounters with him were the most terrifying and monstrous experience I have ever had. I especially remember the glow of his evil red eyes staring at me as he leaned over the foot of the bed where my wife and I were sleeping.

He leaned over the foot of my bed so his red shining eyes were looking down at my face from no more than two or three feet away. He yelled at me in a thundering voice, "I Will Get You!" I Will Get You! I Will Get You! I made a video about Satan's personal attacks on me. The title of the YouTube video is: "Satan Attacks Sacred Child of God." To summarize I have personally experienced many hundreds of spiritual events in my life.

There was a time about 15 years ago a woman whom I knew very well appeared to me in a state of agony. I saw her with my spiritual vision, and she had her clothes shredded as if a sharp clawed animal attacked her. She was screaming from horrific fear and was perhaps only four or five feet away from me. At first, I thought she was in big trouble somehow of her own making and I dismissed her. The next day she appeared to me. Again looking as if part of her hair was ripped out of her scalp, she had a horrific expression on her face and her clothes looked like they were further ripped away from her. However, this time Jesus Christ was with her and slightly behind. Jesus said these words to me, "you need to help her". Instantly I knew she had died and knowing what I did about her life I knew again instantly it was satanic demons that were ripping her clothing and tearing out her hair. She was destined for hell. This was my chance to assist her in going to the heavenly kingdom. I have never seen such anguish and fear inside anybody. But there she was right in front of me with Jesus slightly behind. So, I told her as her particularly good friend, "take the hand of Jesus and he will lead you to heaven." She heard me instantly. Yes, you indeed can talk with beings in the spiritual realm.

She did what I told her instantly and I could see her grasp the hand of our Lord and Savior. The last time I saw her she was holding the hand of Jesus, and they were walking away from me up the path upstairs which led to a beautiful gate. It was the heavenly gate of which there is only one. Because this woman was so terrified by her mother while she was growing up with her sister, I knew she would need a tremendous amount of counseling and psychotherapy. There is more that happened in the story afterward

Booklet #1: CREATION

but that is enough for now. When it comes to the spirit world, I know what I am speaking of.

I ended up authoring a spiritual book that summarized some of my spiritual experiences. The book is titled, "The Divine Resting on My Shoulder." Since that book was published my spiritual experiences have increased greatly.

About 40 years ago I entered into a binding covenant with Our Heavenly Father that is quite simple. I promised I would under no circumstances lie about anything, cheat, or other such terrible sinful things. Looking back, I now realize that was the trigger event that prompted Satan to viciously attack me on three separate occasions in the middle of the night. An incredibly good video was made by my public relations guy, and it is now a nine-minute video on YouTube that describes in detail the horror of the three separate times Satan attacked me. Yes, it was Satan personally. Within the spiritual realm knowing and entity's identity is extremely easy and not prone to error. Now as I write this, every day I am forced to conduct spiritual warfare against Satan himself and his demons. Perhaps five to six or more times each day of my life.

As of now, as I write this for you my life mission has been laid out for me by Almighty God. I think it is wonderful I am so close and intimate with the heavenly Trinity and our Blessed Mother Mary. I am completely humbled Our Heavenly Father has asked me to be his anointed messenger. This is something I never expected in my life at all. But here I am writing wonderful facts about Almighty God so you too will understand much more theology that goes beyond our magnificent Holy Bible.

For more information contact Richard Ferguson via email at:
info@advbooks.com

www.advbookstore.com

www.ingramcontent.com/pod-product-compliance
Lightning Source LLC
Chambersburg PA
CBHW071736040426
42446CB00012B/2375